CW00558109

QUARRIES OF ENGLAND AND WALES

AN HISTORIC PHOTOGRAPHIC RECORD

PETER STANIER

TWELVEHEADS PRESS

TRURO • 1995

CONTENTS

TWELVEHEADS PRESS

First published 1995 by Twelveheads Press,
Chy Mengleth, Twelveheads, Truro, Cornwall TR4 8SN.

ISBN 0 906294 33 9
British Library Cataloguing-in-Publication Data.
A catalogue record for this book is available from the British Library.

Printed by The Amadeus Press Ltd., Huddersfield, Yorks.

CHAPTER ONE
THE PHOTOGRAPHIC COLLECTION

DURING THE PERIOD COVERED by this book (1904-35), the Geological Survey of Great Britain was based at the Museum of Practical Geology in Jermyn Street, Piccadilly, London. In 1935, these two bodies moved to Exhibition Road, South Kensington. They were later incorporated into the Institute of Geological Sciences, which in turn became the British Geological Survey in 1984, with a new headquarters at Keyworth near Nottingham. The museum remains in London. Geological assistants employed by the old Survey were also photographers, and from the early twentieth century they travelled the country extensively, recording rock exposures, landforms and other geological features. Economic geology - mines, pits and quarries - represents an inevitable portion of their photographs.

A distinct photographic unit was later established, and the library of the British Geological Survey now houses a large and unrivalled archive of photographs. Those selected for this book come from the 'A' series of England and Wales, which contains over 14,500 negatives and is still being enlarged. Other series include, for example, the parallel 'B' and 'C' series covering Scotland. A1, the first registered photograph, was taken by J. J. H. Teall, who happened to be the Survey's Director (from 1901 until his retirement in 1914), so it is perhaps no accident that one of his photographs was chosen to start the collection! This particular view, dated 21 May 1904, is of the puddle-trench for the new Howden Reservoir in Derbyshire, so it has some additional interest to the industrial archaeologist. However, the earliest field photograph in the series would appear to be A84, which is of tin mine workings at Cligga Head near St Agnes in Cornwall. It was taken by J. B. Scrivenor in June 1903, and was one of several he made in and around the district in that month. Robert Kidston was also active in September of the same year and his photographs of a marl pit at Wrexham, Denbighshire, are numbered as high as A3822. However, the two photographers with whom this book is concerned are T. Clifford Hall and Jack Rhodes, who took most of the plates illustrated here.

Thomas Clifford Fitzwilliam Hall (1883-1956), having studied at the Royal School of Mines, was employed from May 1903 as a General Assistant, working with John S. Flett in the Petrographical Department where he was also concerned with the photographic work. Flett was working on contributions to the Survey's Memoirs in Cornwall and on Dartmoor then in preparation. Connected with this, a number of Hall's photographs were taken in Cornwall and Devon. Beginning with a series around Falmouth, his earliest was taken on 8 August 1904 of Sunny Cove (A6), and published in 1906 (Hill and MacAlister, Plate VIII). For the photographs chosen here, Hall made visits to Cornwall, Devon, Leicestershire and South Wales in 1904-9. He left the Survey in September 1910, when he was appointed lecturer at the Camborne School of Metalliferous Mining in Cornwall, and his subsequent distinguished career as an economic geologist took him all over the world (Anon, 1958, 72-3).

One of Hall's colleagues was John Rhodes, who had

Trerice China Clay Works, Retew, near St Dennis, Cornwall

Every process is shown in this one picture. We can see the pit and its tip, engine house, launder, micas, pits, tanks, dry, linhay and railway for transport. Even Hall recognised this and included a small sketch plan with his notes. The long clay dry (pan-kiln) and linhay (store) are part of the landscape of the traditional china clay districts. These are slate-roofed, although others had corrugated iron. Clay slurry is passed through micas and round pits before being settled in the five tanks built into the hillside up behind the dry. It is then dug out and spread on the heated floor of the long dry. Blocks of clay can be seen stacked in the openings of the linhay, which is served by a loop siding from the Retew branch railway. The six rail wagons, however, have brought coal for the furnace. Note the tall smoking chimney and its flue from the dry on the left. The view is looking east across the Fal river valley, from the much larger Wheal Remfry china clay works. 57 men were recorded working here in 1906.

T.C. Hall, 4.30 p.m. 25 October 1905 [A166]
SW 927572

worked as a collector and assistant in the Fossil Department since 1881. Other duties involved some photography before his retirement in May 1918. Meanwhile, his son John Rhodes Jnr (Jack) had joined him at the Survey as a General Assistant in 1910, although his career was soon interrupted by the Great War when he served as an air mechanic in the Royal Naval Air Service from 1916 to 1919. Within a year of his appointment, Jack was engaged in photographic work, replacing Hall by printing plates at the Survey for Flett as well as taking to the field. He is the major contributor to this book, and from the evidence gathered it can be seen that he travelled widely on photographic assignments to Dorset (1911-12 and 1930), Kent (1911 and 1921), Yorkshire (1911, 1926 and 1930), Warwickshire (1912-13), Staffordshire (1912 and 1921), Cheshire (1914), Somerset (1922), Lancashire (1923 and 1935), Denbighshire and Merionethshire (1925), Surrey (1926), Durham and Nottinghamshire (1930) and Lincolnshire and Northamptonshire (1933). There is no record of his retirement, but he was down in Devon recording three metal mines and the ball clay workings at Bovey Tracey in 1945, and he went to the Great Weldon stone quarry in Northamptonshire as late as 1949. His photograph of the latter is perhaps the last of his published works (Hains and Horton, 1969, Plate XA).

The early photographers were said to have travelled on occasion on horseback or bicycle, and the carrying of their heavy equipment must have been no small problem. Hall sometimes used a bicycle, this being seen in at least one of his plates. Rhodes had a motorbike and side-car (fitted out to carry his equipment), which features prominently in a picture taken of Haigh House Hill Quarry near Huddersfield in July 1926 (A3582). That October, a car appears in at least three of his Surrey photographs - just a coincidence, or was he proudly including his new acquisition? The same car can be seen four years later at Seacombe Quarry in Dorset.

The two photographers used a half-plate wooden field camera together with glass plate negatives for all their pictures, and Jack Rhodes continued to use glass negatives until at least 23 March 1937 (A7078). The photographs were usually recorded in meticulous detail - the location being indicated by latitude and longitude in degrees, minutes and seconds (the metric National Grid reference system did not come into operation until after 1945), the date, time of day, weather conditions, camera orientation, lens, plate and exposure time. The time of day is often very precise, and where there are several pictures of the same quarry workings, one can almost see the photographer scrambling about choosing a new viewpoint. Brief explanatory notes

Registered Number.	GEOLOGICAL SURVEY AND MUSEUM. BRITISH PHOTOGRAPHS.		Photographer's Number.
166.			*175. T.CH.*

Photographed by *T. Clifford Hall.*

Locality	County	Maps		Latitude
Trerice China-Clay Works, St Dennis.	*Cornwall.*	1 in. *347. 40*	6 in. *SE E.*	*50° 22' 35"*
				Longitude *4° 57' 40"*

SUBJECT OF PHOTOGRAPH

General View of Trerice China-Clay Works.

This view is of particular interest owing to the fact that at these works the juxtaposition of the various processes renders possible, within a small compass, a bird's-eye view of the whole working. The annexed diagram indicates the position of the several parts.

Direction of View	Size of Objects in Foreground	Plate	Lens and stop
Looking E.		*Imp. Ord. Backed.*	*Cook 7.7 F.16.*

Date	Time	Light	Exposure (and Screen)	Destination (For use in Office only)
25. Oct. 1905.	*4.30. p.m.*	*Bright Sunshine.*	*1/4. Second.*	*A.4.*

accompany each photograph in the collection's albums. The example illustrated here is by Hall when working in the Cornish china clay district in 1905.

The photographs' contribution to the study of industrial archaeology is that they record many quarrying and stone-working methods which are no longer practised. Some are especially well composed and a cut above the rest, such as that showing the block being lifted at Seacombe Quarry, which has been caught at just the right moment. Or what could be more extraordinary landscape portraits than the Clogau slate quarry or the excavations at the Erith sandpit? There is the occasional accidental bonus of background information, like the windmill seen above the roadstone Windmill Quarry near Nuneaton. It must be said, however, that there are some very unexciting views, with neither men nor equipment, but they may now be the only record of a vanished industry that once had a major impact on a local community and environment. Other photographs may record the state of roads or railways at the time.

The photographic collection's most notable shortcoming is the absence of the vast slate quarrying industry of Snowdonia, although this is compensated by other archives. Nor are there photographs covering the limestone and gritstone quarries in Derbyshire or the Bath stone industry of Wiltshire. The main reason for this apparent oversight was that the photographers were assigned to record only those districts which were then being surveyed in advance of the publication of a particular Geological Memoir. The national importance of some quarrying districts is therefore not necessarily reflected in this book, as the choice of plates has been confined to those available. The photographs are illustrated here with location maps. All excavated stones, sands or clays are important in their own right, locally or nationally, and to avoid any hint of preference, the photographs of quarries and pits are taken alphabetically. Each plate is accompanied by the photographer's name, date, BGS number and a six-figure grid reference where known.

CHAPTER TWO
QUARRYING IN ENGLAND AND WALES

THE RICH AND DIVERSE geology of England and Wales has been exploited since early times by quarrying which is one of the great primary industries upon which we depend for raw materials. Arguably, quarrying dates back to the Neolithic period, albeit on a very minor scale. Although surface stones were used for most prehistoric monuments, very few actual quarries - rather than stone taking sites - have been identified, but one is the stone axe factory site high up on the slopes above Great Langdale in Cumbria. Quarrying on an organised 'industrial' scale was first developed by the Romans, who were great users of stone, for buildings, monuments, tombs and roads. The Jurassic freestones in particular came to their notice (Blagg, 1990). Anglo-Saxon quarrying was limited (Jope, 1964), but the stone industry revived in the great period of church and cathedral building of the Middle Ages (Parsons, 1990) and continued thereafter for both public and private buildings.

The third age of stone quarrying came with the Industrial Revolution, when industry and commerce created new demands for building stones for factories, housing and many public works and civil engineering projects. Improved transport systems, particularly the canals and railways, enabled remoter quarries to be opened up to compete in wider markets than hitherto possible. Roadstone quarries were a new type which made great advances in the nineteenth century, increasing in scale and developing so that 'modern' methods were well established by the time of the first photographs in this book. While these quarries have continued to expand dramatically to the present day,

'dimension' stone quarrying has declined in the face of competition from cheaper materials such as reconstituted stone and reinforced concrete.

Igneous, metamorphic and sedimentary rocks and deposits have all been quarried or dug for building, engineering, monumental and decorative stone, kerbs, setts, roadstone, lime, cement, brick, tile or pottery making.

Brick clays are used here in a general sense for all clays, marls and shales which have been dug for bricks, roofing and flooring tiles, pipes, pottery and earthenware in many parts of England and Wales.

Chalk is prominent in south-east England, where it has been quarried for many purposes, but here we see it being worked for making cement and burning for agricultural and building limes in Kent and Surrey.

China clay or kaolin, resulting from the decomposition of granite in Cornwall and west Dartmoor, has been widely exploited for the paper and pottery industries. China stone is a less altered form and has been quarried as a building material and for the porcelain industry. The same granite of south-west England has yielded a valuable dimension stone, worked into large blocks of great strength for building, civil engineering and monumental work. Other granites of England and Wales are less important nationally, but it is worth noting that the 'C' series of the BGS collection has a number of fine photographs taken by W. D. Fisher in June 1939 of famous Scottish granite quarries in Aberdeen and Kirkudbrightshire.

Ironstone was excavated over many years in vast opencast

pits in Northamptonshire, Leicestershire and Lincolnshire, feeding the blast furnaces around Corby and Scunthorpe. Although strictly 'mineral' rather than stone working, they are akin to quarrying and are therefore included here by way of contrast.

Limestone is one of the most useful rock types quarried today, for building stones, roadstones and aggregates, lime, flux and cement. It is distributed widely in England and Wales (especially the former) as well as through geological time. Of the chosen limestones, the Silurian is limited in distribution but the Carboniferous is important for roadstone in the Pennine areas of Yorkshire, Derbyshire and Durham, the Mendips of Somerset and in south Wales. Although the Permian limestones of north-east England were worked for building stone, the photographs emphasise their use for lime-burning. The most important building limestones are the Jurassic freestones which are found in a belt traversing England from Dorset to Yorkshire. The quarrying of Portland stone on its small island is so well documented in photographs that it is treated separately in this book.

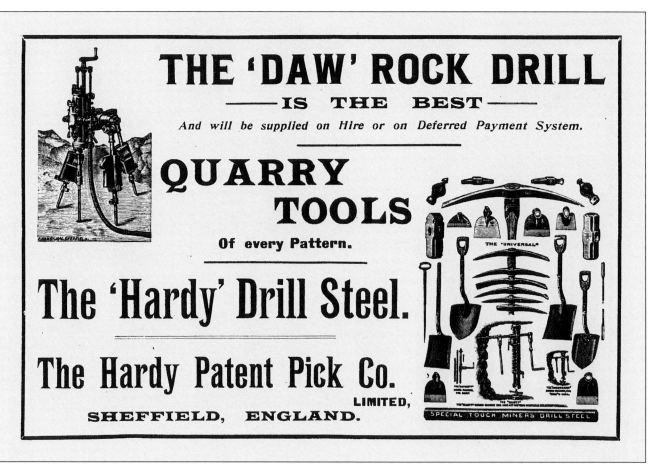

Roadstone and aggregate quarries are now the largest and commonest types today, worked in the hard igneous and metamorphic rocks of upland England and Wales, while other important sources include sandstones, gritstones and the Carboniferous limestones.

Sand and gravel is worked from pits in mostly Tertiary and later glacial and alluvial deposits. According to its make-up, sand can be used for mortar, glass-making and foundry moulding sand. Gravel is important for roadstone, concrete aggregate and artificial stone. Tin streaming on the Cornish moors, another form of gravel working, is represented in the BGS collection although not in this book.

Sandstones of different ages are important building stones in many parts of Britain. We see here sandstones from the Millstone Grit and Coal Measures of the Carboniferous in Yorkshire, the New Red Sandstone (Triassic) of the West Midlands and Cheshire, and the Lower Greensand (Cretaceous) of the Weald in Surrey.

Metamorphic slate has been quarried in western Britain to produce millions of roofing slates, as well as slabs for flooring, cisterns, tables and lintels. Examples of quarries in north Wales, south-west England and the Lake District are given here.

THE WORKING OF QUARRIES AND PITS

The word 'quarry' is derived from the Latin quadrare, to make square. Quadraria were places where squared stones were cut, which is another way of saying an excavation in beds yielding large 'dimension' or 'block' stone for all building and monumental purposes. 'Freestone' is a term normally applied to those certain limestones or sandstones which can be cut and carved easily in any direction. Strictly, 'quarry' should be confined to where such stone is produced, but by common usage it has come to mean any hard rock excavation, which today more than often includes workings for crushed aggregates or roadstones. A 'pit' is not necessarily shallower, but refers to the extraction of less consolidated

materials such as clays, sands, gravels and even chalk rock.

The form taken by a quarry or pit is closely related to the geology and the purpose for which the material is sought. The working methods witnessed in this book are still basically traditional, with mechanisation only just appearing. In the freestone quarries, techniques had remained largely unchanged since medieval or even Roman times. Witness, for example, the workers at Ham Hill or Linby, still using what are essentially ancient quarrying methods well into the twentieth century.

Any large quarrying operation should be well planned, with the establishment of a face with stepped terraces or benches from which the work proceeds downwards to avoid dangerous undercutting. This has not always been the case in reality, and just prior to the Great War some operators were being criticised for their 'rough methods' where 'soft rocks, such as sand or chalk, are too often worked in a manner which is as unscientific as it is dangerous.' The usual reply of these quarriers was that any systematic method was rendered uneconomical by their low-value product, a belief which had no foundation (Greenwell & Elsden, 1913, 152).

All quarrying involves the removal of overlying strata of poor quality rock, which must be set aside and back-filled as part of the operation. This overburden can be of a considerable depth; in some Portland quarries it has been economical to strip off as much as 50 feet (15 metres) to reach the prized stone. Elsewhere, a good hard bed above the stone might be left as a roof when the quarriers resorted to underground working.

Stone mining, or underground quarrying, has take place at a surprising number of places throughout England and Wales. Mining for stone dates back to the Neolithic period when high quality flint for tools was mined from shafts and galleries in the Upper Chalk. Of several known sites in south-east England, Grimes Graves in Norfolk is the most extensive with over 80 acres (37 ha) of shafts and pits. The Romans may have been involved in mining for building stone in a small way, as at Beer in Devon, but most stone mines date from the medieval period onwards. As with the surface quarries, the nineteenth and twentieth centuries saw considerable developments underground. Although the famous Bath freestone mines and Snowdonian slate mines cannot be included in this book, there are views of underground workings in the Purbeck district of Dorset.

MACHINERY AND EQUIPMENT

Methods of stone extraction are as different as the geology, and we see variety in the plates illustrated here. In the dimension stone quarries there are simple hand tools, such as picks for channelling at Ham Hill, bars for levering at Shackstead Lane and Linby, swell jumpers for boring at Longdowns, or scales and wedges at St Paul's, while mechanisation includes the steam channelling machines at Higher Bebington and Bowers quarries. All these quarry types use drills and wedges to exploit the natural joints and bedding wherever possible. Blasting with small charges of black powder in carefully positioned holes may be used to shake large blocks from their bed without damaging them. For the winning of roadstone, however, more powerful explosives in deep boreholes are essential to shatter the rock from the quarry face, in preparation for further reduction by machinery. The latest in steam drilling equipment is seen at Dosthill and Prospect quarries. Extraction methods for the miscellaneous sand, gravel, clay or ironstone pits range from shovels and spades (at the simplest level) to water hoses and giant steam excavators.

Stone-breaking by hand was employed in the early or small roadstone quarries, and it was reckoned that a good man could break about 3 cubic yards (2.3 cubic metres) of limestone or as little as half a cubic yard (0.4 cubic metres) of granite per day. As late as 1913, some road engineers were said to still prefer hand-broken stone for macadam because stone-crushing machines were considered to produce a less angular product.

Stone crushers are illustrated at Gwavas, Hailstone and Tregargus quarries. Based on the Blake jaw crusher, they could be worked by a portable steam engine or a fixed stationary oil engine. This early type was invented by E. W. Blake of Newhaven, Connecticut, USA, and introduced to England by Marsden of Leeds in 1860. A development was Hadfield's patent jaw crusher, using manganese steel for the jaw face. There were also crushing rolls and gyratory crushers, chosen by quarriers to suit the particular needs of their stone. The largest jaw crushers could deal with about 150 tons (152.5 tonnes) per hour, tiny in comparison with modern gyratory crushers which have a capacity of 2,000 tonnes per hour. The crushed stone was graded or sized when fed into the upper end of an inclined cylindrical rotary screen or 'trommel' which had sections perforated with holes of progressively larger sizes. Graded stones fell through into storage bins below, while any over-sized stones passed out of the cylinder and were returned to the stone-breaking machine. Crushing and screening plant became larger when quarry operations increased in size, as well seen in the overall view of Jee's Quarry works.

CRANES AND EXCAVATORS

The cranes seen working in the stone quarries range from the earlier timber hand-derricks, well illustrated at Beaudesert and Longdowns, to larger steam or electric-powered lattice steel derricks in the quarries of Portland and Crosland Hill.

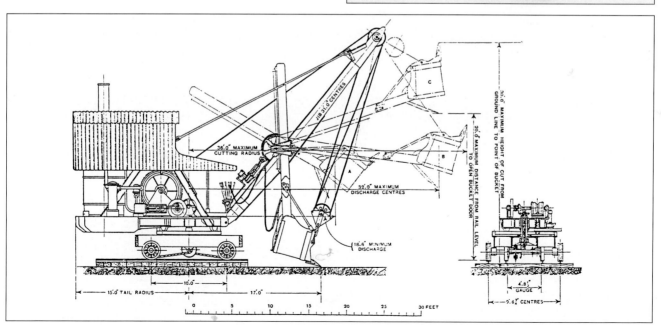

COULTER & CO.,

BANK FOOT FOUNDRY, BATLEY,

YORKS.

Sole Inventors and Makers of the ONLY Successful Patent

Stone & Marble Dressing & Moulding Machine.

The Simplest and most useful machine yet offered to Quarry Owners, Masons, or Contractors. Each Machine will do the WORK OF 10 MEN. SAVING 75 PER CENT. of the simple cost of working the stone, or will save its whole COST in 12 MONTHS, or even less.

Considerably over 500 Machines at Work.

Dressing all kinds of stone from the hardest to the softest, working plucky stones to full length, and not leaving sharp arris, and run all kinds of plain mouldings.
Guaranteed to work ordinary hard grit stone at 1d. per super foot, 180 super feet per day of 9 hours
An Ashlar Step 6ft. by 12in. by 8in. can be dressed in one hour on all four sides ready for fixing.

→ ILLUSTRATED CIRCULAR, WITH FULL PARTICULARS, ON APPLICATION. ←

MAKERS OF PATENT STONE-SCABBLING MACHINES.

Mechanical excavators show a range of development, from the superb steam excavator removing gravel overburden in a Swanscombe chalk pit to the monster machine powering away to uncover the ironstone at Dene Pit near Corby.

POWER FOR THE QUARRIES AND STONE WORKS

Steam was an important source of power at many quarries, but waterpower was utilized wherever possible. See, for example, the waterwheels pumping water from the great Delabole slate quarry, and the waterwheel for working the dressing machinery at the Deeside Slate slab works. The granite quarry at De Lank had a large turbine. Many smaller

quarries of the twentieth century relied upon a stationary oil engine for driving compressors and dressing plant.

STONE DRESSING MACHINERY

Whatever the source of power, the types of stone dressing machinery illustrated here include stone saws (circular at Delabole and Wynne slate quarries, vertical at Ham Hill, and horizontal frames at Portland). We also see rotary slate trimmers at Wynne and a planing machine working on Portland stone. The skill of the stone mason himself is shown at Portland too.

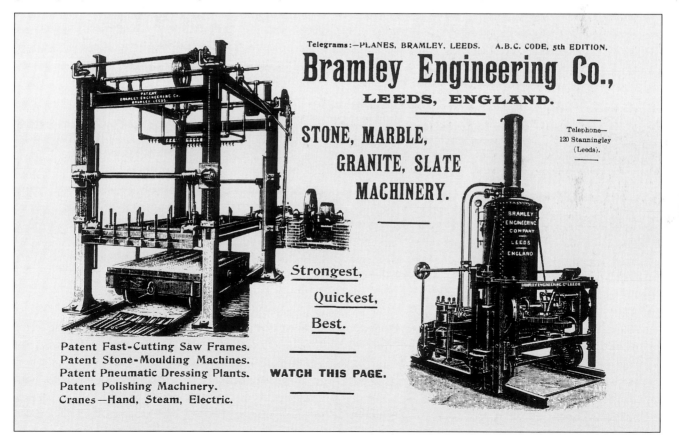

Telegrams:—PLANES, BRAMLEY, LEEDS.   A.B.C. CODE, 5th EDITION.

Bramley Engineering Co.,
LEEDS, ENGLAND.

Telephone—
120 Stanningley
(Leeds).

STONE, MARBLE, GRANITE, SLATE MACHINERY.

Strongest,

Quickest,

Best.

WATCH THIS PAGE.

Patent Fast-Cutting Saw Frames.
Patent Stone-Moulding Machines.
Patent Pneumatic Dressing Plants.
Patent Polishing Machinery.
Cranes—Hand, Steam, Electric.

TRANSPORT

Transport represents a significant proportion of the final cost of all stone products. It is a vital part of any extractive industry, and examples of road, rail, canal and sea transport are given among the photographs. Many quarries could not have been developed on the scale they did without railways, whether as direct sidings, branch lines or private quarry tramways.

Within a quarry or pit, the most basic method of moving material was by wheelbarrow, as at Caldey Island or Kirmington, while other photographs show a variety of types of internal quarry tramways, ranging from small clay pit tracks and inclines for tubs to standard gauge sidings (both seen at New Howley Park). Temporary trackwork was necessary because layouts would be constantly changing as the quarry face advanced. This is shown at Callow Hill Quarry, where the more permanent main track is laid with heavier rails than the temporary branches. Points were crude on the smaller tracks, and were often lifted over by hand or the employment of a well-placed boot. Light iron or steel rails were usually flat bottomed so they could be spiked directly into stone blocks or timber sleepers. 'Jubilee' track, dating from late Victorian times, was prefabricated with metal sleepers in sections of straights, curves and points, and there are examples at the Worth and Callow Hill quarries.

More lengthy tramways took quarry products away to shipping piers (as at Gwavas and Porthoustock on the Cornish coast) or wharves beside canals or main line railways, for onward carriage to destinations many miles away. Jee's Quarry at Hartshill, Warwickshire, had a complex internal system feeding the crusher, screens, washing plant and the canalside loading wharf. Maps show the tramway systems of this and nearby quarries feeding the Coventry Canal or main line railways. Some longer mineral lines were railways in their own right. The Deeside Tramway was an interesting line with over 2 miles (3.2 kilometres) of timber trackway along its 3-mile (4.8 kilometre) course as it descended inclines to a wharf beside the Llangollen and Corwen Railway. The gauge here was 2 feet 7 inches (0.79 metres). Direct sidings of varying lengths from main line railways are seen, for example, at De Lank, Ifton, New Howley Park, Portland and Crockham Hill.

The photographs show a variety of types of rolling stock. The smallest are the tubs in the clay pits at New Howley Park or Ruabon. Tubs of this size could be hand-pushed, but larger wagons were horse-drawn, as at Swanscombe and Long Harry Mine. There is a fine detailed view of a Deeside Tramway wagon, showing the screw-type braking system used when descending the inclines by gravity. Steam locomotive power is seen (just) at the Stonepit House ironstone pit, where it was just part of a very large railway system. At Worth, note

a small Simplex-type locomotive.

Canals were used for transport by some Midlands quarries. Roadstone could be carried cheaply for many miles, although the small size of barges restricted the potential of this traffic. The wharf for Jee's Quarry at Hartshill is shown beside the Coventry Canal. The quarry company even owned a few barges and stone was sent as far as Oxford and Banbury via the Coventry and Oxford Canals. Hailstone Quarry at Rowley Regis was near the Dudley Canal, to which it was connected by a tramway incline. In that same area, the Wrens Nest limestone quarries were served direct by canal branch tunnelled beneath the hill. The view of the Doulton Basin on the Dudley Canal shows the apparatus for tipping the clay tubs into the waiting narrow boats. Elsewhere, the Pen-y-bont brickworks had a tramway to the Shropshire Union (Ellesmere) Canal as well as a siding from the Great Western Railway's Shrewsbury and Chester line.

Road transport was still rather poorly developed at the time of the photographs, but there are good contrasts, including the horse and cart at the small Carne Quarry in Cornwall, the heavy traction engine with trailers on Portland, Dorset, and the petrol lorries seen at Nore Hill in Surrey and Skegby in Nottinghamshire.

Kirmington Brick Pit, Lincolnshire

This photograph is a particularly good one showing a corner of a small hand-worked brickpit. The section includes late glacial sand and gravel (for which the pit was also worked) above about 18 feet (5.5 metres) of interglacial warp clay. The lowest bed is clean sand, seen in the excavation between the two men. Steps in the clay face behind show how the pit has been steadily deepened by spadework. This pit caused a small stir in geological circles in 1903-4 when its bed of estuarine clay was shown to lie between two glacial deposits, and the result of a 96-foot (29 metres) borehole was reported to the British Association's meeting at Cambridge.

Jack Rhodes, September 1933 [A6315]
TA 103115

CHAPTER THREE
BRICK CLAYS

CLAYS, MARLS AND SHALES of marine or freshwater origin occur in many geological periods from the Devonian to the most recent glacial and alluvial deposits. These are widespread throughout England and Wales, where they have been dug in pits for bricks, roofing and flooring tiles, pipes, pottery and earthenware. Notable are the beds in the Coal Measures (Carboniferous), the Keuper Marls (Triassic), the Kimmeridge and Oxford Clays (Jurassic) and the Reading Beds and London Clays (Eocene).

Brickmaking is especially important and the source beds may provide the main building material in some areas. Elsewhere, bricks have rivalled stones where the two are found close together. Traditionally, bricks were manufactured close to the pits to minimise the cost of transporting the bulky, low-valued clay. Likewise, markets for bricks were limited by carriage costs, with the exception of 'specials'. Shales, mudstones and siltstones of the Coal Measures produce durable bricks, but of a deep red colour. The so-called 'Accrington Bloods' of Lancashire were not to the taste of Alec Clifton-Taylor (1972, 233), who considered Accrington to have 'the dubious distinction of having made some of the most durable and visually disagreeable bricks in the country.' Harsh words, indeed! Another hard red brick was produced at Ruabon, Denbighshire, along with tiles. Terracotta was

significant in the period 1880-1910 when the area became known as the Terracotta Town. J. C. Edwards was the largest terracotta producer in the world. Henry Dennis was also important.

Most counties had brickworks in the past, but the industry has seen great rationalisation since the 1930s. The brickmaking industry has become dominated by massive pits and works around Bedford and Peterborough, where the carbonaceous content of the Oxford Clay reduces the amount of fuel needed for firing their 'Fletton' bricks. Further economies are achieved here because the extensive deposits allow for large-scale working. These, with improvements in transport and other factors, have enabled the bricks to be marketed far away to the detriment of local brickmakers.

Special clays include fireclays from the Carboniferous Coal Measures, their high alumina content making them important for firebricks and refractory purposes such as blast-furnace linings. Cornwall is an unlikely place for bricks, but firebricks were a speciality in association with the china clay workings. These were also produced at Lee Moor in Devon. The Etruria Marls of the Upper Coal Measures make especially hard, strong and damp-resistant engineering bricks which were once produced in great numbers. 'Staffordshire Blues' were made around the North Staffordshire coalfield and potteries, and in the Black Country coal and iron district

of the south. Advantage was taken of the Staffordshire & Worcestershire Canal to carry these bricks to Stourport on the River Severn and elsewhere.

As well as bricks and tiles, the Etruria Marls of the north Staffordshire Potteries produced common earthenware. The greater value of potters' clay allows this raw material to be transported in bulk for greater distances. Apart from china clay, which is still taken to the Potteries, high quality potting clays include the ball clays, which are worked in mines and open pits near Wareham in Dorset. These estuarine deposits belong to the Bagshot Beds (Eocene) and were carried here by rivers from kaolin sources further west on Dartmoor. Ball clays from a similar source were deposited in former lakes in the Bovey Tracey and Petrockstow basins of Devon, where they are also worked from pits and mines (Messenger, 1982). Jack Rhodes photographed the Bovey Tracey workings in August 1945, too late to be included in this collection.

Botcherby clay pit, near Carlisle, Cumberland (now Cumbria)

The view shows the method of cutting laminated clay with spades. Note the baulks left in the partly flooded pit, and the loaded tram wagon on the crudely-laid track. Flooding in the pit was relieved by a small pump, which is seen in photograph A2288. The Botcherby brick and tile works was located about 1¼ miles (2 km) east of Carlisle.

Jack Rhodes, August 1922 [A2287]
NY 425559

Jobern's Clay Pit, Vigo, Walsall Wood, Staffordshire (now West Midlands)

A claypit in the Etruria Marls, worked by Joseph Jobern & Co. for manufacturing blue bricks, tiles, drain-pipes and other products. The deposit contains bands of conglomerate and breccia ('Espley' rock), piles of which can be seen discarded on the right. The heavy wheelbarrows are pushed from the working areas along planks, and tipped into a skip wagon hidden in a chamber at the foot of the incline. Note the small pumphouse behind the men and the smithy(?) above. Both are clad in timber - there is no corrugated iron here. At the top of the incline we see a substantial winding house and the brickworks. Maps show a short tramway to the Daw End Branch canal. The pit lies just south of Walsall Wood, where Joberns Holdings Ltd were still producing blue and engineering bricks, coping, etc in the early 1960s.

Jack Rhodes, 10.30 a.m., 9 October 1912 [A1538] SK 050023

Stourbridge Glazed Brick works, Blowers Green, Dudley, Worcestershire (now West Midlands)

This print is of superb quality and shows old types of round downdraught kilns at the Thornleigh Works of the Stourbridge Glazed Brick & Fire Clay Co. Ltd. Loading and firing them in the kilns is the final production stage after digging, weathering and moulding the clay, and drying the 'green' bricks. The fuel is coal. These beehive-type kilns were easier to control and therefore preferred by manufacturers of higher quality wares. Photographs A1982-6 show other views of the works, including a new kiln fired by gas made in a furnace on the site. The firm was still here in 1961, making glazed and firebricks.

Jack Rhodes, 11.20 a.m., July 1921 [A1981] SO 935892

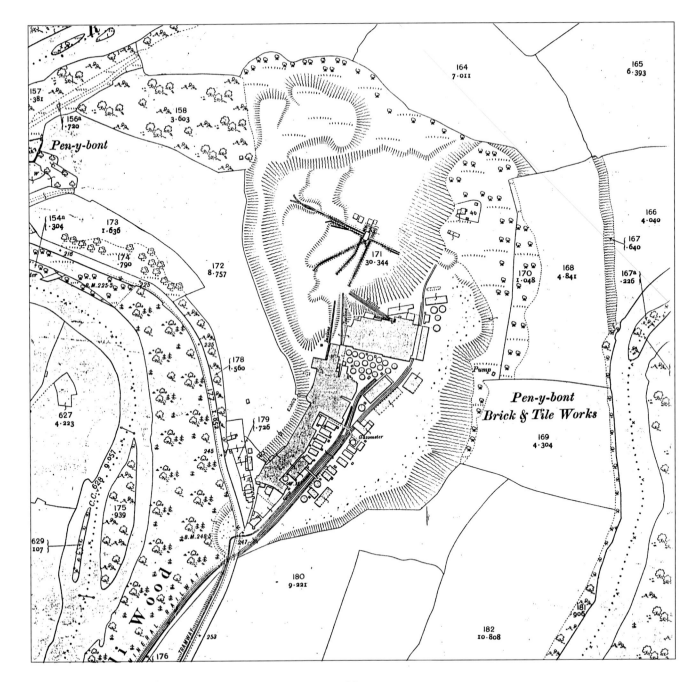

Pen-y-bont

Pen-y-bont
Brick & Tile Works

Gasometer

Pump

Pen-y-bont Clay Pit, near Cefn-mawr, Denbighshire (now Clwyd)

Looking west over a much larger operation, about ³/₄ mile (1.2 km) south-east of Cefn-Mawr, near Ruabon. Brick clay is being worked in the lower part of the purple Ruabon Marl. The various raised tramways are of interest here. Material quarried in the background is brought to the screening plant, from which it is then trammed in skips out along the raised tramways and tipped onto stockpiles below. From here it is loaded into skips and taken to the works. Pen-y-bont was established in 1865 and J. C. Edwards produced his famous terracotta ware here. There was a private tramway to the Shropshire Union Canal at Irish Bridge and a parallel siding to the Great Western Railway. Today, the pit is still worked but the marl clay is sent away to manufacturers in various parts of England.

Jack Rhodes, July 1925 [A3166] SJ 292417

Ruabon Brick & Terracotta Co's Pit, Ruabon, Denbighshire (now Clwyd)

A pit worked for bricks and terracotta ware in the lower part of the Ruabon Marl (a purple marl with thin bands of greenish-white sandy marl in the Upper Coal Measures). This view, looking south-south-west, shows many tramways branching to the working face from turntables, which are fixed plates upon which the clay 'tubs' can be turned with ease. The tubs are typical of clay pits, being small enough to be pushed about by hand. The pit could be either at Gardden or the Tatham Works, both being worked by the firm at this date. The Ruabon Brick & Terracotta Co. Ltd. was still making quarry tiles, fittings, bricks and sills in the early 1960s. Today, Messrs Dennis Ruabon at Hafod are the only producers of quarry tiles in Wales.

Jack Rhodes, July 1925 [A3164] location uncertain

New Howley Quarry brickworks, Morley, Yorkshire

The shale overlying the Thornhill Rock at the sandstone quarry (page 101) is used here for making red bricks. Men can be seen digging the brick clay at various points, but the floor of the shallow pit has apparently reached the hard sandstone. A man in the centre foreground is working a compressed air drill - a pipe can be traced back to the long cylindrical air receiver to the right of the incline. The shed above may be the compressor house. The radiating tramway rails have been laid across widely spaced timbers which act as sleepers. These temporary tracks are always changing, so the flat iron plates are more convenient than special turntables for positioning the tubs at the foot of the incline where they are attached to the endless chain haulage system. Men at the top of the incline are waiting outside the Howley Park Brickworks for the next loaded tub. Note also the rail-mounted steam crane handling stone blocks.

Jack Rhodes, July 1926 [A3617] SE 262255

Lee Moor Brick and Tile Works, Torycombe, Devon

The Lee Moor area on the western flank of Dartmoor was developed extensively for china clay after the 1830s, along with brickworks, pan-kilns, tramways and a workers' settlement. The Lee Moor brickworks was begun by William Phillips in the 1830s and enlarged after Martin Bros. took over in 1862. Discoloured clay was mixed with coarse waste for making bricks, tiles and pipes. These included firebricks and tiles for the floors of pan-kilns. This fine view looks east over the works. The square brick chimney stack on the left is surrounded by four round kilns of downdraught type, constructed externally in local granite. The tallest chimney serves continuous kilns. Note the drying and mixing sheds, and the tiled roofs in the foreground. In the background are the smoking chimneys of pan-kilns, with their settling tanks on the slope above. Men can be seen loading bricks onto railway wagons brought into the works on sidings from the 4 feet 6 inches (1.37 metres) gauge Lee Moor Tramway (1858-1947) which took china clay down to shipping wharves at Plymouth. The brickworks closed in 1943 but the clay industry still forms a huge complex today. Similar brickworks, such as at Carbis (BGS photographs A219-220), existed in the Hensbarrow china clay district of Cornwall.

T. C. Hall, 1 p.m., 1 August 1908 [A712]
SX 571612

Doulton Basin on the Dudley Canal, Netherton, Worcestershire (now West Midlands)

Transport is vital to all extractive industries. Here in the heart of the Black Country, the Dudley Canal and its branches curved through clayfields and collieries - a complex of pits, depressions, dumps, tramways and mineral lines, some of which served canal-side wharves. The Doulton Basin was at the north end of a double-tracked incline which ran for 1,600 feet (488 metres) from the Saltwells Clay Field, worked by Doulton & Co. (Rhodes called this 'Doulton's Clayhole'). This view, looking north, shows the basin wharf used for transferring clay to canal traffic. The men are about to tip clay into a narrowboat (the lad is standing on one end) beneath one of two rotating tipping frames which overhang the basin. A loaded boat is moored on the far side. Note the simple pointwork of the tramway. The head of the incline is just behind the camera position. The small bridge in the background carries the towpath of the Dudley Canal (passing at right angles behind) over the basin entrance. The site, just west of High Bridge, is now part of a housing estate and Saltwells Wood is a nature reserve.

Jack Rhodes, 12.20 p.m., July 1921 [A1957]
SO 936877

Whinney Hill Quarry, near Accrington, Lancashire

The new pit of the Accrington Brick & Tile Works, working the Accrington Mudstone in the Lower Coal Measures. This was a good clay for making strong engineering bricks, for which Accrington was a notable centre of the industry in Lancashire. The view is rather murky, but the main points of interest are the steam navvy hard at work in the distance and the double incline in action with an endless chain of skips. The overhead ropeway in the background is part of a colliery system. This clay pit is one of two just east of Clayton-le-Moors.

Jack Rhodes, August/September 1923 [A2650]
SD 756304

No. 4 Pit, Milton Street, Swanscombe, Kent

This photograph, looking south-west, shows the method of working the chalk for cement making. A tunnel has been excavated into which tramway wagons can be drawn, and a vertical pipe has been cut through the chalk down to the tunnel and lined with timber. Thus, as the chalk is worked away (by pickaxe) from the top, it is fed into the chute and the crude trap at the bottom controls the fall of the rubble down into the waiting wagon. Steps on the chute allow workmen to climb up and down. Note also the safety ropes. Flints are included in the horizontal bedding of the chalk, which is clearly seen in this view. Such pits appear to have been worked on a large scale, in a planned and systematic manner. Quarrying became fully mechanised in later years and Rhodes's photograph A7864 shows an excavator working at Frindsbury (Rochester) in August 1939, with the chalk being loaded onto a train drawn by a steam locomotive at a lower level. The marks made by the excavator's shovel are prominent in the evenly-bedded chalk face (Gallois, 1965, Plate VIIA).

T.C. Hall, 12.15 p.m., 15 March 1906 [A227]
TQ 595744

26

CHAPTER FOUR
CHALK

CHALK IS A PURE FORM of limestone of the Cretaceous period. Its main outcrop sweeps across south-east England from east Devon to the Lincolnshire and Yorkshire coasts. From the hub of Wiltshire's Salisbury Plain, the North and South Downs march east into Surrey, Sussex and Kent. where they enclose the older beds of the Weald. There are Lower, Middle and Upper horizons, and most chalk has been quarried for roadmaking, lime-burning and the manufacture of Portland cement, as well as for whiting and a furnace flux. Kent is a major chalk quarrier, and the other important counties include Berkshire, Buckinghamshire, Essex, Hertfordshire, Lincolnshire, Surrey, Wiltshire and Yorkshire.

Harder varieties of chalk stone known as 'clunch' have been quarried for a building stone over centuries; the Totternhoe stone quarry in Bedfordshire was re-opened for this in 1982. A small quantity of chalk has been mined in Berkshire, Hertfordshire and Kent, while Beer Stone is an important variety of building quality which has been worked underground in east Devon since Roman times.

The excavation of chalk has a long history. In the Neolithic period, flint from the Upper Chalk was mined on something approaching an 'industrial' scale as a raw material for axes and other tools at sites as widely dispersed as Grimes Graves (Norfolk), Cissbury (Sussex) and Easton Down

(Wiltshire). More recently, this by-product of chalk quarrying has been used for buildings, roadstone and gunflints, as well as being ground for the pottery industry.

The photographs are confined to chalk pits for cement and lime in the North Downs of Kent and Surrey. In Kent, chalk for agriculture and building was quarried from slopes overlooking the Thames estuary back in medieval times, but the nineteenth century saw a dramatic expansion of activity due to cement manufacturing. The district between Dartford and Gravesend was a perfect location for that industry's development, being at the boundary of the raw materials of chalk and clay. River mud from the Thames and Medway was used at first, being brought in by barge. In 1796 James Parker of Northfleet patented a process for manufacturing Roman cement. Portland cement was patented by Joseph Aspdin in 1824, and his son William established a cement works at Northfleet Creek in 1847 (a bottle kiln is still preserved here at the Blue Circle Heritage Centre). In 1825 James Frost built a cement works at Swanscombe, which John Bazley White took over eight years later. By the 1890s there were at least sixteen cement works between Gravesend and Stone. Associated Portland Cement Manufacturers Ltd was formed in 1900, bringing together five Northfleet manufacturers and J. B. White & Bros of Swanscombe. The subsidiary British Portland Cement Manufacturers Ltd of 1911 included more local firms in Stone and Greenhithe. By the late 1920s, White's Swanscombe works and Bevan's Northfleet works were the only two in the district. The former became Britain's largest cement manufacturer and exporter before closing in November 1990. Today, Blue Circle Industries' Northfleet works continues in operation, supplied from Eastern Quarry, Swanscombe, which is one of the largest chalk pits in England. London Clay is pumped to the works in a slurry beneath the Thames from Ockenden in Essex.

In Surrey, the outcrop of the North Downs chalk narrows at the famous Hogsback ridge between Farnham and Guildford before continuing east past Dorking, Reigate and Oxted. There were once many chalk pits, mostly cut into the scarp-face for marling, lime-burning, building and roadstone. Harder 'clunch' chalk was excavated as a building stone in medieval times from beneath Guildford. Chalk is almost synonymous with lime-burning in Surrey, and the grey Lower Chalk has been worked for this purpose most notably at Betchworth and Brockham (Dorking Greystone Lime Ltd) just east of Dorking. The Lower Chalk produces a hydraulic lime, and 'Dorking Lime' was used, for example, for the Houses of Parliament and Nelson's Column in London. Cook's Dorking Greystone Lime Works was recorded at work in at least 1623. The 'Brockham Kiln', a continuous type of kiln, was first devised by Alfred Bishop at Brockham in 1889. The Dorking Greystone Co. also had extensive works at Betchworth, burning Lower and Middle Chalk for lime in the 1930s. There were other large chalk pits at Reigate, Merstham and Oxted. The Merstham Greystone Limeworks were developed in the early nineteenth century by the famous contractors Jolliffe and Banks, who promoted the Croydon, Merstham and Godstone Railway of 1805. This was also an area where 'firestone' and 'hearthstone' were worked by drift mines from the Upper Greensand which lies beneath the chalk (Sowan, 1975).

Steam navvy removing gravel overburden at No. 4 Pit, Swanscombe, Kent

The overburden is being loaded into a horse-drawn wagon. A superb posed photograph showing steam navvy No.100, an early type with a fixed jib and a pivoted bucket raised and lowered by a chain. It has double-flanged wheels and its own set of broad-gauged rails. There is a driver, engineer and a man to operate the bucket release, beside whom tallies for 53 loads have been chalked onto the base of the jib. Having been positioned, the horse waits patiently with its driver during the loading operation. The horse has a collar and trace harness to haul the short wheel-based tipping wagon. Lying at 100 feet (30 metres) O.D. and known as the Implementiferous or High Terrace gravels, the overburden was of value and quarried for its gravel content before the underlying chalk was exposed. The former name is derived from the Palaeolithic hand-axes and other tools found therein, a more common occurrence in the days of hand-excavating when the workmen could spot them more easily.

T.C. Hall, 1.10 p.m., 15 March 1906 [A232] TQ 597745

Barnfield Pit, Swanscombe, Kent

Fifteen years after the previous pictures, Jack Rhodes recorded this hand-operated monitor water jet being used to remove the overburden before working the chalk for manufacturing Portland cement. The remaining sandy beds are only about 6 feet (1.8 metres) deep here, so this rather novel method is being tried in preference to a mechanical excavator: a messy business. Elsewhere in England, hydraulic monitors were more usual in the china clay pits of Cornwall and Devon where they are still used today. This part of Barnfield Pit (South) was close to the No. 4 Pit and the view looks north to show in the background houses along Knockhall Road and the walled Ingress Gardens behind the face of Knockhall Pit.

Jack Rhodes, 1.30 p.m., April 1921 [A1901] TQ 595746

Dorking [Greystone] Limeworks, Surrey

Surrey is best known for its chalk and limeworks. Lime was said to have been burnt here 'for several hundred years' by the time this photograph was taken. The view, looking north-west, shows three limekilns for making Dorking lime. These are flare kilns which were charged and emptied between each firing; the central kiln burns, while that on the right is being discharged. In common with many Surrey limekilns, they have domed tops. Similar kilns are shown here at Dorking in a sketch by G. Scharf dated 1823 (Williams, 1989, 23). Note also the skip wagons and turntable, and the fuel supply on the extreme left. This fine photograph was first published in Dines and Edmunds (1933, Plate IVB).

Jack Rhodes, May 1929 [A4633] TQ 160503

30

Greystone Lime Quarry, Merstham, Surrey

Looking north-west across the Merstham Lime Co's chalk pit and limeworks, this view shows old domed limekilns still in use for burning the grey marly Lower Chalk. There are three lower kilns and eight higher kilns, one of them smoking heavily. The chalk pit was near the terminus of the Croydon, Merstham and Godstone Railway, an early plateway of 1805, which passed beyond the kilns. The standard-gauge railway in the foreground was a siding laid from the London to Brighton Railway in 1841. Note also the LMS wagon at a higher level Having been filled with refuse for eleven years, the site was destroyed when the M23 motorway was constructed through here in 1972.

Jack Rhodes, May 1929 [A4636] TQ 295542

Lantern China Clay Pit, near Rescorla, Bugle, Cornwall

This is a typical small china clay pit of the period, looking north-east. The single-track incline is for hauling waste wagons from sand pits at the base to the surface by a wire rope from a winding engine beyond; an empty wagon has just been lowered into the pit. On the right at the top men are tipping back towards the pit, suggesting that space here was at a premium. Clay-laden water pumped up from the pit (note the engine house with two pumps at the shaft on the left) is carried to drags and micas situated behind the tip. The smoking chimney of the clay dry is also seen. Lantern was an old pit, worked at least back in 1858 when Messrs. Lovering and Martin produced 300 tons of potting clay. It was among 52 pits in Cornwall and Devon to be closed by ECLP in 1942, leaving work concentrated at just seventeen. The overgrown pit and works still survive, beside the B3374 about 1¼ miles (2 km) south-south-east of Bugle.

T.C. Hall, 16 October 1905 [A174] SX 025570

CHAPTER FIVE
CHINA CLAY & CHINA STONE

CHINA CLAY OR KAOLIN is not sedimentary like most clays, but has been formed within parts of the granites of south-west England. It is a result of the process of kaolinisation by which feldspar crystals in the granite have been altered or decomposed to form the clay kaolinite.

Since its properties were discovered around 1746, china clay has been worked in most of the granite districts in Cornwall and Devon. This activity has had a far greater impact on the Cornish landscape than any other quarrying industry, producing huge open pits and the characteristic white conical 'sky-tips' of quartz sand and unaltered feldspars - the 'Cornish Alps' of the Hensbarrow or St Austell district, which is the still the headquarters of an industry which produces around 3 million tonnes of china clay each year. In addition to Cornwall, Lee Moor on western Dartmoor (Devon) is still an important source, and there were once workings further out on the moor at Redlake (Wade, 1982). The clay was first sought for the manufacture of fine pottery, and then also for paper and sizing cotton goods. Today, around 80 per cent is used as a filler and coating in paper-making, with some taken by the pharmaceutical, paint and plastics industries. The development of the Cornish industry has been well documented (Barton, 1966), while the history and processes of the industry are shown at the Wheal Martyn china clay

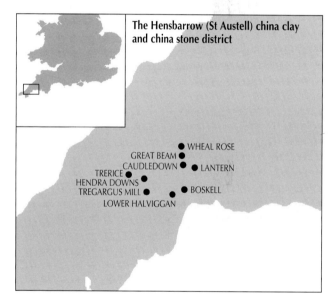

The Hensbarrow (St Austell) china clay and china stone district

WHEAL ROSE
GREAT BEAM
CAUDLEDOWN
LANTERN
TRERICE
HENDRA DOWNS
TREGARGUS MILL
BOSKELL
LOWER HALVIGGAN

museum near St Austell.

By the time of these photographs (1905), the industry had been established for a century and a half. To open a china clay pit, the overburden and iron-stained material was first removed and dumped to one side, mostly by hand. The kaolin-bearing material was washed from the face by water diverted into the pit via leats from a stream. The water formed a gully or strake, leaving behind unaltered rock (stent). The loose material was washed to the bottom of the pit where traps collected the coarser quartz sand which was later dug out and hauled in self-tipping wagons up an incline to the top of a tip. The stent had to be removed from the pit as well. The clay-laden water was pumped via a 'button-hole launder' to the surface where it flowed through long 'drags' which separated and deposited the finer sand and mica. The clay slurry was then thickened to a creamy consistency in settling pits and tanks which were usually behind a long pan-kiln or dry where the clay was spread on a tiled floor which was heated by flues running beneath. The dried clay was stored in the adjacent linhay, from which it was loaded into road or rail wagons; the better grades of clay were packed in barrels. The long low drys with a tall chimney at one end are still a characteristic feature of the clay districts. These traditional processes and their surviving archaeology are clearly explained by Smith (1992).

A network of tramways, railway branches and sidings was developed, especially around Hensbarrow, for transporting the finished clay products. All the clay was, and still is, sent to other parts of the country and abroad, mostly by sea from the main ports of Charlestown, Par and Fowey. Pentewan was a fourth port in the Hensbarrow district, served by its own railway in 1829-1918 (Lewis, 1981), but the harbour became silted, ironically by china clay waste.

Although there had been a successful experiment in the 1870s to wash the clay from the pit face with a water jet from a fire engine, high pressure monitors (as seen in the Barnfield chalk pit, Kent) did not become widespread until after the photographs in this collection. Their automated successors are still in use today. Indeed, all the processes are basically the same except that modern techniques are applied on a grand scale.

The striking landscape is now being replaced by more massive tips using modern methods and earth-moving equipment, for up to 8 tonnes of waste, overburden, quartz sand, unaltered rock, feldspars and mica must be disposed of to produce one tonne of fine clay. The industry in Cornwall and Devon is dominated by ECC International, which has grown out of amalgamations beginning in 1919 with the formation of English China Clays Ltd, and later English Clays Lovering Pochin and Co. Ltd (ECLP).

The photographs have been selected from around sixty views taken by Hall in October 1905. They capture the state of the industry perfectly at the start of a century which was to see immense developments and changes in the industry.

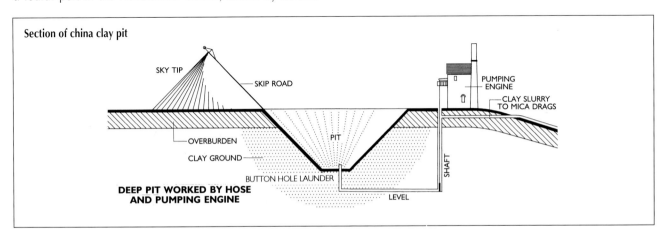

Section of china clay pit

SKY TIP
SKIP ROAD
PUMPING ENGINE
CLAY SLURRY TO MICA DRAGS
OVERBURDEN
PIT
CLAY GROUND
SHAFT
BUTTON HOLE LAUNDER
DEEP PIT WORKED BY HOSE AND PUMPING ENGINE
LEVEL

Lantern Pit sand pits

Clay workers attend the Lantern sand pits. Soft material is being washed from the stope or working by a stream of water flowing down a gully (strake) into the boarded sand pit at the bottom of the works. Heavier sand particles settle while the clay-laden water flows off over the lower boards and down into the sump to the button-hole launder seen standing on the right, through which it is pumped to the surface. This sand pit is almost full. The front boards of the lefthand pit have been removed so it could be dug out and the sand loaded into wagons for hauling up the incline. Note the Cornish shovels; the man in the strake is helping break up the material with a short pick, or dubber.

T.C. Hall, 1 p.m. 16 October 1905 [A175]
SX 025570

Lantern pump and engine house

Seen at the top of the pit in photograph A174, is this engine house for a small rotary steam engine working two pumps in the shaft on the left. Note the very greasy crank. Clay-water is raised from the pit to the short wooden launder in the foreground which carries it to the drags and micas, the first of which are seen in the right hand corner of the photograph.

T.C. Hall, 11.30 a.m. 16 October 1905 [A176]
SX 025571

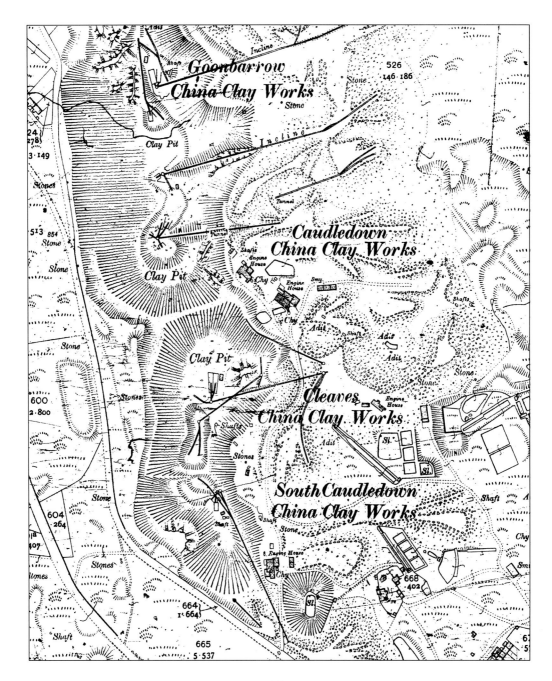

Caudledown China Clay Works, Goonbarrow Downs, Cornwall

A general view looking north over workings about a quarter of a mile (0.4 km) in length. Three separate companies were working this extended pit. From the foreground are the South Caudledown, Cleaves and Caudledown china clay works. The two Cornish engine houses (for pumping and winding engines) and their boiler houses belong to this last. Flatrods working pumps in the pit can be seen rising from the South Caudledown section to a third engine house which is just outside the picture on the right. The most distant workings are of the Goonbarrow china clay works.

T.C. Hall, 12.30 p.m. 10 October 1905 [A168] SX 008578

37

Great Beam clay works, Bugle
  Men clearing out the mica drags with scrapers, looking east.

T.C. Hall, 4.15 p.m. 10 October 1905 [A182]

Lower Halviggan china clay works, St Mewan
  The men are emptying a settling tank, loading two wagons on a temporary track laid into the pan kiln behind. Looking north-east. (Hall called this 'Alviggan')

T.C. Hall, 9 November 1905 [A199]

Wheal Rose clay works, near Bugle, interior of dry or pan-kiln

A wagon brought through a hatch from a settling tank is seen on a travelling bridge, for distributing clay slurry on the heated tile floor of the long narrow dry. The clay has been marked out in blocks before it is fully dry to enable it to be lifted out into the linhay on the right.

T.C. Hall, 2.30 p.m. 17 October 1905 [A186]

Boskell china clay works

Outside the linhay, men are packing casks with china clay.

T.C. Hall, 11 a.m. 10 October 1905 [A205]

The Purple Quarry, Hendra Downs, Nanpean, Cornwall

Looking north-east inside a china stone quarry. China stone is being quarried, making use of joints in the rock, so there is little need to resort to gunpowder for loosening blocks. Note the tramway, men and tools including swell jumpers for drilling holes to break down the larger blocks. Hendra was an early site for china stone. The name of the quarry is derived from the type of china stone worked here.

T.C. Hall, 3.30pm 24 October 1905 [A212]
? SW 9556

CHINA STONE

China stone ('petuntze') is only a partly kaolinised form of Cornish granite. It was quarried as a building material in the past, being easier to cut and carve than the solid granite. However, the significant discovery of its qualities at Tregonning Hill in the 1740s led to its use for quality porcelain, as a glaze or in the body of the pottery. The valued types of china stone are Hard Purple (whitish with purple fluorspar and unaltered feldspar), the softer Mild Purple and the soft White, while the Buffstone is stained with iron oxide and considered waste. China stone has been quarried between Nanpean and St Stephen in the west part of the Hensbarrow china clay district. It was quarried in a similar manner to the unaltered granite, but it was then broken, at first by hand and later by stonebreaking machines.

The potters preferred to grind the highest grade of china stone themselves, but the lower grades were ground in Cornwall in waterpowered stone-grinding mills often located in the valleys below the quarries. Any pieces with mineral staining were removed to prevent discolouration of the pottery, before the remainder was loaded into water-filled grinding pans at the mill. The waterwheel worked rotating arms in the pans by means of shafting and gearing, and the resulting slurry was settled and dried in pan-kilns similar to those used for china clay.

Tregargus Mill China Stone Quarry, near St Stephen

Here, the men are about to tip quarried china stone blocks into a jaw-crusher, from which crushed stone will spill down the chute into the wagon parked beneath. The tramway leads off to the china stone mills. The timber and iron-strengthened bodies of these wagons swivel, to tip sideways or at the end. A small steam or oil engine is housed in the shed on the right and drives the crusher by a belt hidden under the sloping corrugated iron cover. Note that wagons are hauled up the short incline (built of china stone blocks) by a cable engaged on the right; crude but effective. Note also the pick marks in the quarry face behind, indicating the relative softness of the stone here.

T.C. Hall, 3 p.m. 20 October 1905 [A214]
SW 949541

Tregargus china stone grinding mills, near St Stephen

On the west side of a narrow valley, half a mile (0.8km) north-east of St Stephen-in-Brannel, there were five china stone mills with waterwheels, each taking water from the one above. A tramway served a sixth waterpowered china stone mill at Trevear, across the valley. Looking north, with the upper part of Tregargus Quarry behind, the photograph shows the No 2 mill in the foreground. The iron overshot wheel was built in 1896 by F. Bartle & Sons of Carn Brea and measures 35 feet by 5 feet (10.7 x 1.5 metres). It was the largest of the wheels and drove six circular grinding pans, three in each of the flanking buildings. Here, china stone lumps were ground to a slurry when pushed around in water by revolving arms in the pans. Photograph A217, which shows the interior, and another of this wheel being erected have been published elsewhere (see Major and Watts, 1977, Plates 76-79). This photograph also shows the 22-foot (6.7 metre) diameter wheel turning at the No 3 mill, with the building of No 4 mill above that. Thomas Olver & Co were here from the time of the photograph until closure in about 1960. The No 2 wheel was the only one to be saved when these fascinating mills were sold for scrap in 1968; the quarries above have been infilled with waste which is encroaching upon this site.

T.C. Hall, 2 p.m. 20 October 1905 [A216] SW 949539

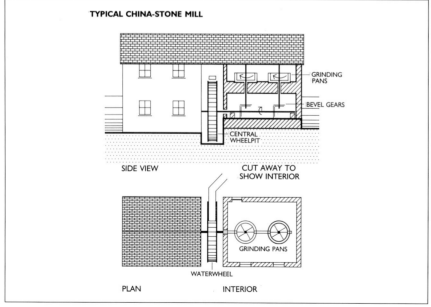

TYPICAL CHINA-STONE MILL

GRINDING PANS

BEVEL GEARS

CENTRAL WHEELPIT

SIDE VIEW

CUT AWAY TO SHOW INTERIOR

WATERWHEEL

GRINDING PANS

PLAN

INTERIOR

CHAPTER SIX
GRANITE DIMENSION STONE

GRANITE AS A TERM for strength and durability has been applied to many hard stones and greatly misused to advantage by owners of roadstone quarries wishing to enhance the sales of their product. However, true igneous granite is found at relatively few places in England and Wales, and granite good enough to be a dimension stone has an even more limited distribution. The principal area is in south-west England, where large granite bosses were intruded in a molten state beneath cover rocks of slates and shales about 280 million years ago, and subsequently revealed by erosion to form the spine of the peninsula. This 'silver-grey' granite is characterised by the main crystals of glassy quartz, white feldspar and brown or white mica. The feldspars are usually the most prominent. China clay and china stone are altered forms of granite, covered by photographs on the previous pages. Although Dartmoor (Devon) is the largest granite district, most quarrying activity was in Cornwall and concentrated in Carnmenellis where the principal firm was John Freeman, Sons & Co. Ltd. of Penryn (Stanier, 1986). Bodmin Moor was also quarried for a medium-grained granite and views of the famous De Lank Quarry are included here.

Although 'moorstones' had been taken from the upland slopes in prehistoric times, and many more were used by medieval church and bridge builders, actual quarrying did not

begin until the early nineteenth century. Widely spaced joints enabled large blocks of the tough granite to be extracted for building and civil engineering projects, and the product of the quarries was exported from Penryn and other ports for bridges and public buildings in London, and docks, dockyards, breakwaters and lighthouses in Britain and even abroad. As the century progressed, monumental work also became important. The photographs shown here were taken when the industry was just past its peak, when competition from Scandinavia was already having an effect.

In the Cornish granite quarries black powder inserted in a hand-bored vertical hole was sufficient to lift a mass from its 'bed' or horizontal joint without damaging the stone. Large blocks were cut down to size by inserting plugs and feathers in a line of small holes, and then squared up with a chop axe or patent axe. As seen in the first photograph, it was common for some of the stone to be dressed in the quarry itself, although there were large workyards at places such as Penryn and De Lank.

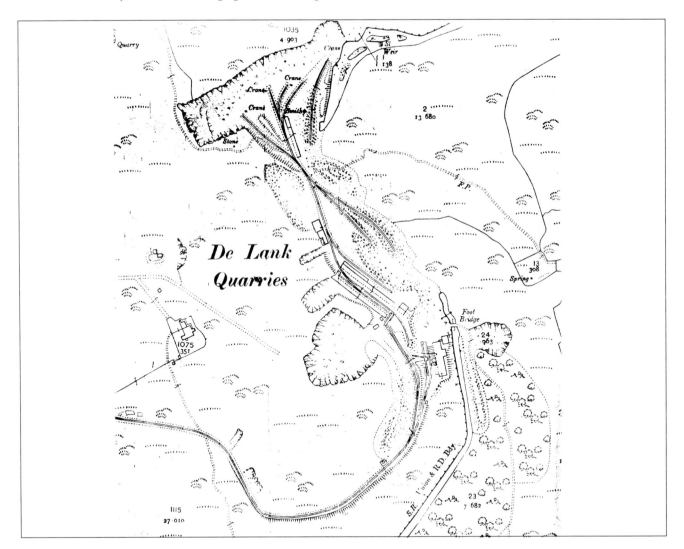

De Lank Granite Quarries, St Breward, Cornwall

A general view of this very well-equipped granite quarry and works, looking north from across the De Lank gorge. This famous quarry on the north-west side of Bodmin Moor was connected by a 1½ mile (2.4 km) siding from the Wenfordbridge terminus of the Bodmin and Wadebridge Railway (London & South Western Railway) in the early 1880s. Of two inclines, the shortest can be seen here with a railway wagon at its foot. Above the incline, the long run of dressing sheds can be seen in front of the main quarry workings. On the left is the Eddystone Quarry, source of granite for James

Douglass's lighthouse when it was built in 1878-82. Twenty years later, the Beachy Head lighthouse also came from here. Other De Lank granite towers include the Smalls and Bishop Rock lighthouses.

At the lower level in the foreground, a siding serves a works containing two 7-blade saw frames and ten polishing machines, supplied by Henderson Bros. of Aberdeen, in addition to a large lathe for turning granite columns. Finished memorials and a locomotive crane are visible. The smaller building to the right is the compressor house. A small plant crushes and grades waste tipped down a chute from the dressing yard above, and a railway

wagon waits to be loaded. Note the iron pipe for the turbine on the right.

The quarry had been fitted-out by Hugh Shearer during the Eddystone contract, but at the time of this photograph his works had been inherited by the De Lank Granite Co., owned by the Hard Stone Firms Ltd. of Bristol. The same view today would show some traces of the incline and later works in the foreground now being tipped over. The modern dressing sheds are close to the quarry in the background, where activity continues today.

T.C. Hall, 24 September 1907 [A515]
SX 102753

The main upper workyard at De Lank

This view, looking west-north-west, shows part of the main workyard, some 330 feet (100.6 metres) long. On this east side, stone masons are at work in the bankers, open-fronted to allow circulating air to remove unhealthy granite dust. The heavy timber structure supports one rail for two overhead travelling cranes (20-ton steam and 10-ton hand), for handling the heavier loads. A 3-ton steam locomotive crane is also working in the background, while a rough block has arrived on a tram wagon from the quarries behind. Finished stone awaits despatch in the centre of the yard. On the other side of the yard were three dressing machines by J. Spencer & Co. of Keighley (Brunton & Trier's patent). BGS photograph A519 shows a pneumatic surfacing machine or 'dunter' at work on a granite block in one of the open sheds (see Stanier, 1985, Plate 8).

T.C. Hall, 24 September 1907 [A517]
SX 102753

Power for De Lank

This 200 n.h.p. Vortex turbine was made in 1887 by Gilkes & Co. of Kendal. It had a 130-foot (40 metres) head of water, delivered in a 24-inch (0.6 metres) diameter steel-rivetted pipe from a short distance further up the De Lank river. The turbine drove all the machinery at the lower level via a grooved rope pulley of 3ft (0.9m) diameter, companion pulleys and shafting. It also drove a double Cornish tandem air compressor (by Holman Bros., the well-known mining equipment manufacturers of Camborne, Cornwall), the air being used to power three 15-ton cranes in the quarry, rock drills, the smiths' fires and machinery in the carpenters' shop. The compressor house is on the left, standing on a substantial wall. Although it remained here until the 1960s, this turbine was replaced in 1927 by three Gilkes turbines and Broom & Wade compressors erected in a power house further downstream.

T.C. Hall, 24 September 1907 [A520]
SX 103752

Quarry at Longdowns, near Penryn, Cornwall

Typical of many smaller granite quarries in the Penryn district, showing the joints to good effect. The timber mast-crane is also typical, hand-worked with a fixed jib, the whole supported by perhaps six wire or chain guys radiating from the mast-top to anchor points on the quarry edge. The crane is about to lift a large block using a chain sling and pair of 'dogs'. An exposed vertical borehole can be seen in the face behind the lefthand 'dog'.

Blocks for engineering or architectural work are being worked upon, and there are also wooden templates and some tools. A swell jumper (for drilling small holes in a line for splitting the granite blocks) leans against the face behind the lefthand figure. Just in front of him is a chop axe, once the main tool for reducing a granite surface to a 'single axe' finish, but long since considered obsolete in other districts. This is the earliest photograph in this book, and one of the earliest taken for the Geological Survey by

whom it was first published (Hill and MacAlister, 1906, Plate IX). Although not named, Hall located the photograph at ¹/₄ mile (0.4 km) north of Longdowns, 50°10'20"N and 5°9'20"W where it could be one of several quarries which lie close together around a hilltop. The view is looking north-east.

T.C. Hall, 1.30 p.m. 25 August 1904 [A20]
SW 743345

Dene Pit, north-east of Corby, Northamptonshire

Only about 1½ miles (2.4 km) away, but a total contrast to Longhills Pit. The ironstone lies too deep to be reached by hand-quarrying, so a huge steam excavator is stripping overburden from the face and depositing it on a waste heap on the left. Compare this monster with the antiquated type removing gravels in the Swanscombe chalk pit (page 29) to see the great advances made since 1906. The machine is working hard, and black smoke billows over the top of the pit and away across the countryside beyond. It dwarfs a much smaller excavator which is digging the ironstone after it has been loosened by blasting at the bottom of the pit. This will be taken away by rail, and in the foreground men are laying a track which will be extended as the face advances. On the right, the working face exposes the Lower Estuarine Clays and yellow sand overlain by a little Lincolnshire Limestone and Boulder Clay. As with all the ironstone pits, these workings have been back-filled and restored to farmland as the face progressed, which makes the exact location and orientation of the camera especially important. This view is looking north-west. By 1963 the face was reported to be over 1¼ miles (2 km) long but is now abandoned.

Jack Rhodes, August 1933 [A6312] ?SP 915905

CHAPTER SEVEN
IRONSTONE

JURASSIC SEDIMENTARY IRONSTONES ARE no longer worked but the pits were so extensive that they cannot be ignored. The main producing counties were Northamptonshire, Leicestershire and Lincolnshire. The beds also yield limestones which were worked for a metallurgical flux in the blast furnaces as well as a building stone in and around the locality.

The three main Northamptonshire ironstone areas were around Corby (the most important), Kettering and Thrapston. Here were the most extensive and richest of the British Jurassic ores with an iron content of 30-33 per cent. They could be extracted easily by opencast methods and millions of tonnes of ore were obtained from thousands of acres of opencast pits. Iron ore was also mined, notably to the west of Thrapston. Some iron ore was probably worked by the Romans, and certainly since at least the eleventh century, but it was not until 1852-3 that attention was turned again to the Northampton Sand Ironstone. Excavations were begun in the Corby district in 1882. Blast furnaces were built here in 1910 by the Lloyds Ironstone Co. Taken over by Messrs Stewarts & Lloyds ten years later, this was followed in the 1930s by a basic steel plant which specialised in making steel tubes.

The Corby area was a leader in mechanised ore-winning, ever since 1895 when Lloyds Ironstone Co. was the first firm

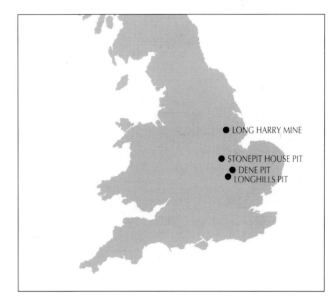

in the country to use mechanical excavators (steam navvies) for working ironstone. Nearly a dozen were at work in the district by 1913. The first electric excavator was used at Corby in the 1930s and, twenty years later, large walking dragline excavators were developed for stripping overburden. The first was at Priors Hall South Pit, which had over 100 feet (30 metres) of overburden covering up to 9 feet (2.7 metres) of oolitic ironstone. These machines later grew to become some of the largest of their type in the world. The use of machinery on such a scale created acres of 'hill-and-dale' landscape where the overburden was deposited behind the working face. Unlike the shallower hand-worked pits, it was especially difficult to restore this land afterwards to agricultural use.

In Leicestershire, iron ores were worked around Holwell, where the 'bump and hollow' landscape results from subsidence of underground workings. Narrow gauge lines from the ironstone pits joined the standard gauge main line at exchange sidings at Cottesmore, near Oakham (now the Rutland Railway Museum). The early photograph here is of an opencast at Wartnaby near Melton Mowbray. To the north east, workings at Eaton and Eastwell continued until the 1960s.

In Lincolnshire, some pits were being worked on a grand scale by 1920, when an account gives us an idea of the extent of mechanisation at the Frodingham Ironstone Mines around Scunthorpe. About 500 men produced a million tons of ore here every year, assisted by twelve cranes for stripping the overburden and a further seven steam crane navvies for excavating the iron ore after it had been drilled and blasted. Despite this mechanisation, about 100 men were still employed to work the pit by hand. The pit at Frodingham was noted for the length and straightness of its face, and the whole was served by fifteen steam locomotives and 700 wagons on 25 miles (40 kilometres) of standard gauge track connected to the Great Central Railway (Livens and Barnes, 1920, 814-5).

Working methods above and below ground have been described by Hollingworth and Taylor (1951, 55-65). The following plates from the three counties show activities of great contrast.

Longhills Pit, east of Corby, Northamptonshire
The working face, looking west. The lower Estuarine and Lincolnshire Limestone lie above the Northamptonshire ironstone, the lowest bed in the photograph. At its thickest development, ten beds of shelly oolitic limestones overly the Northampton Sand ironstone to a depth of 45 feet (14 metres). A number of dark patches seen along the face are 'gulls' (fissures) filled with limestone rubble and chalky Boulder Clay. These glacial features, which lie parallel to valley sides, are clearly of annoyance to the quarriers. Limestone (for flux) is being quarried by hand along the whole face in small benches along the natural bedding of the stone. Note the face ladders and small corrugated iron shelters for the workmen. It must have been a skilled job barrowing waste over the planks supported on trestles to the tips on the right. Wagons at the far end of the railway track below have been loaded with ironstone. This pit was worked by Stewarts & Lloyds Minerals Ltd.

Jack Rhodes, August 1933 [A6304] ?SP 910890

Stonepit House Pit, near Wartnaby, Leicestershire

This is a much earlier view, looking east across the Stanton Coal & Iron Co's workings. Middle Lias ironstone is being stripped or 'bared' of a heavy covering of Boulder Clay. The surface of the ironstone slopes towards the camera, so the overburden is being worked in a second bench as its depth increases. Note the men clearing overburden for barrowing across the plankways for tipping on the left. Below, each man has his own railway wagon to fill with ironstone. At least nine wagons are being loaded; the fourth and fifth from the camera have been stacked very high. A small steam locomotive is just visible on the extreme left. First published in Lamplugh, *et al* (1909, Plate I).

T.C. Hall, 11.15 a.m. 26 September 1908
[A720] SK 714234

Long Harry Mine, Greetwell, Lincolnshire

One of the mid-Lincolnshire ironstone mines at Greetwell, with both opencast and underground working. The site is surprisingly close to Lincoln, just 1¼ miles (2 km) to the east. A bed of the Lincolnshire Limestone helps make the roof over the ironstone and it is possible to work underground. Looking north, a pony pulls a train of six laden wagons from one of two mine entrances. Note the dumb buffers and the use of a breast harness, more suited to underground work than the harness arrangement seen at the Swanscombe chalk pit. Pit props wait ready for use and the inevitable dog looks on. The average height of the working face was 8 feet 6 inches (2.5 metres) and about 1 foot (0.3 metres) of ironstone with a high phosphorus content was left as a floor in the mine. A similar thickness was left in the roof whenever possible (Hollingworth and Taylor, 1951, 79-80).

Jack Rhodes, September 1933 [A6319]
TF 003724

Wren's Nest Hill Limeworks, near Dudley, Worcestershire (now West Midlands)

Here on the west side of Wren's Nest Hill, the shaft gives access to the lower band of Wenlock Limestone (locally called the Dudley Limestone), a small Silurian inlier which was worked underground here and on the east side of the hill. The Wren's Nest Tunnel of 1805-37 extended from the Dudley Canal's Castle Mill Basin to below the works in this photograph. The dip slope of the middle limestone shales is on the right, from which the upper limestone band has been quarried. A steam winding engine on the left serves the shaft. Note the 'rattle chain' for winding and the boiler. The tramway wagons are iron-sided for handling lime; behind, horses and carts stand above a pair of limekilns. Part of this interesting scene survives on the edge of a nature reserve. The engine house has gone and the shaft is fenced but the two brick-built limekilns are in good order, with datestones of 1902 and 1903. Nearby are the remains of four horseshoe limekilns, characteristic of this district.

Jack Rhodes, 12.35 p.m. July 1921 [A1966]
SO 935918

52

CHAPTER EIGHT
LIMESTONE:
SILURIAN, CARBONIFEROUS
AND PERMIAN

THE OLDEST LIMESTONE DEPICTED here dates from the Silurian period and has a limited distribution. Near Dudley in the West Midlands, an anticline has formed a small but important outcropping ridge of Silurian limestone (Wenlock series) which was worked all around Wren's Nest Hill and underground too in large caverns for buildings, lime-burning and as a flux for the Black Country iron industry. The underground quarries were connected by shafts and canal tunnels. The same limestone was mined at Hay Head Lime Works at Aldridge near Walsall, and served by the Daw End Branch of the Wyrley & Essington Canal, built in 1800.

Carboniferous limestone, however, is one of the most important of the limestones and is found in south Wales, the Mendip Hills of Somerset and the Pennines of Derbyshire, Yorkshire and Durham. It does not lend itself well to masonry and stone dressing, but it has been quarried for lime-burning and cement-making, and has become a major source of aggregates and roadstone. For this limestone, the two contrasting examples of quarries given here are from opposite ends of south Wales: Ifton Quarry in Monmouthshire (now Gwent) and Caldey Island off the coast of Pembrokeshire (Dyfed). Carboniferous limestone was quarried along the south part of Pembrokeshire, where much was burnt either in

the district or was shipped across the Bristol Channel to limekilns on the coasts of north Devon and Cornwall. The BGS collection has examples of these quarries and limekilns, such as at Tenby, Ludchurch and Llandebie (Carmarthenshire). The photograph of High Cliff Quarry on Caldey Island shows one such source of stone for the kilns on the mainland.

53

Underground at Wren's Nest Hill, east side

Rhodes used a five-minute exposure to get this dramatic picture of the huge sloping caverns cut in the lower band of the Wenlock Limestone. The roof of Wenlock shales is supported by pillars of uncut limestone on the right. The view is looking north and shows the dip of the rock well and is typical of the underground quarries which riddle this district. Stone from beneath Dudley Castle Hill, for example, was carried away by canal boat from the Castle Mill Basin through Lord Morley's Tunnel of 1778. Later cuts from the basin were the 2,942-yard (2,691 metres) Dudley Tunnel (1792) and the 1,227-yard (1,122 metres) Wren's Nest Tunnel (1805-37). Today, boat trips take visitors into the tunnel, mine chambers and the Castle Mill Basin which is now open to the sky.

Jack Rhodes, July 1921 [A1964] c.SO 938917

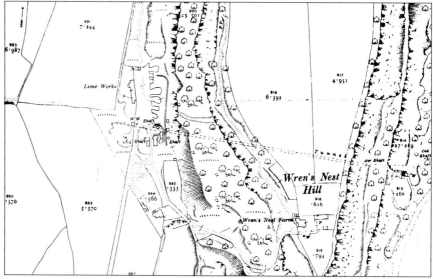

Ifton Quarry and limekiln, Rogiet, near Chepstow, Monmouthshire (now Gwent)

A quarry in Carboniferous limestone, where broken stone is used for roadstone and to feed the large steel-plated cylindrical limekiln which dominates the view. Fuel and limestone are fed to the top of the kiln by the inclined bridge. The lime plant shed can be seen at the bottom of the kiln. Near the incline is a portable steam engine, although its purpose there is unclear. A vertical boiler behind the timber wall supplies steam via pipes to drills at the rock faces. There was a ³/₄ mile (1.2 km) siding from the Great Western Railway at Severn Tunnel Junction Station, and the quarry branches are in the process of re-arrangement on the right. Two almost identical rail-mounted steam cranes with short jibs are seen working at the end of a line of railway wagons. The main geological interest here (and the reason for the photograph) is that grits are found infilling hollows and fissures in the Carboniferous limestone; overlying this is dark Trias material, first worked back from the quarry edge. At the time of the photograph the Ifton Limestone Co Ltd was employing around 60 men here. The Ifton Quarries and Lime Works (1935) Ltd produced fluxing stone and roadstone until at least the 1960s. This section of the quarry has been infilled, but another part was being worked by ARC South Wales in 1994.

T. C. Hall, 31 January 1909 [A801] ST 463886

High Cliff Quarry, Caldey Island, Pembrokeshire (now Dyfed)

This photograph is included to show that it was worth quarrying Carboniferous limestone on an offshore island, 2 miles (3.2 kilometres) south of Tenby. Operations have worked back from the natural cliff face, with quarried stone gathered at the bottom of the scree slopes. The men are loading barrows from one of these stock-piles, then wheeling them along planks out of the picture to the right. The three small solid-wheeled barrows are flat in order to carry the larger rough blocks. Their destination would seem to be a place by the shore for loading small sailing vessels for onward transport to the mainland, probably for lime-burning. High Cliff is on the north side of the island, sheltered from the prevailing south-westerly winds. The view looks west and the mainland can be seen in the background. It is interesting that the photograph was taken in the same year the island was bought by a Benedictine Brotherhood led by Dom. Aelred Carlyle.

Stone from the quarry was used to build the Caldey monastery in 1910-13. There was much investment, with new equipment and a short tramway to a jetty for loading small coasters. High Cliff Quarry closed in 1921-22 when Carlyle's community failed in financial debt.

T. C. Hall, 14 July 1906 [A315] SS 145971

PERMIAN (MAGNESIAN) LIMESTONE

The Permian Magnesian Limestone occurs in a narrow belt about 5 miles (8 kilometres) wide from Nottinghamshire to the Durham coast. It has been quarried extensively along this outcrop for building stone, roadstone and lime-burning. It is a dolomitic limestone where carbonate of magnesium has replaced carbonate of calcium. The Lower Magnesian Limestone was prized as a building stone in the medieval period when it was used for major religious buildings such as York Minster, Beverley Minster, Selby Abbey and the Great Tower at Fountains Abbey. In the nineteenth century, Royal Commissioners chose magnesian limestone from Bolsover Moor (Yorkshire) and Mansfield Woodhouse (Nottinghamshire) for the Houses of Parliament, with further

Linby Quarry, near Hucknall Torkard, Nottinghamshire

Lifting out a slab of stone, using two heavy quarry bars. The man on the right is knocking stones beneath the slab every time it is raised further, to support it and open up the gap. Note the rake, part of the equipment for clearing the working area. The face is in the Lower Magnesian Limestone, with quarrying aided by near-horizontal beds of varying thicknesses. Vertical boreholes can be seen in the lower part of the face, suggesting that some blasting has been used to open up this shallow quarry. The quarry, described as about 2 miles (3.2 km) north of Hucknall Torkard, was worked for walling, small building stone, paving flags and lime-burning. The small pieces of stone stacked in the foreground might be used for random walling, but the thicker slab being extracted would have a greater value. Photographs A5031-4 show ornamental work executed in Linby Stone. This stone is still produced for building work, by Abbey Quarries Ltd.

Jack Rhodes, July 1930 [A5030] SK 535522

stone brought in from North Anston when those sources ran out. However, little attention was paid in the quarry to the selection of the best stone. Because of its dolomite content, this stone can weather poorly in polluted atmospheres and there were most unfortunate consequences. It is still quarried for restoration work.

Several of the quarries photographed here are around Mansfield Woodhouse (one of the famous areas), just north of Nottingham. Other BGS photographs in the same region include Lindley's quarries at Mansfield, working red and white dolomitic sandstones in 1911 and 1930.

The northern limit of the Permian Magnesian Limestone is in County Durham, where some of the stone is a true dolomite, with over 40 per cent magnesium carbonate. The main quarries are between Coxhoe and Mainsforth, where it has been worked as a refractory material for the iron and steel industry, as well in the pharmaceutical, glass and textile industries.

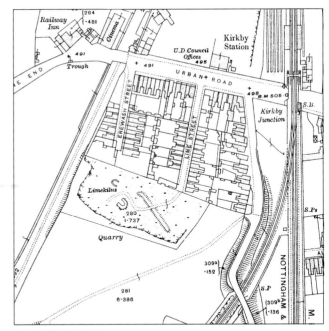

Lime Street Quarry, East Kirkby, Nottinghamshire
Another quarry in the Magnesian Limestone, showing similar horizontal beds. The quarry appears to be worked in a small way, close to the village. Note the pile of quarried stone (for local building?) and the broom for cleaning the face. The view is looking north-east, and the end of Lime Street enters the quarry in front of the semi-detached house behind the pile of stones. The quarry is shown on the 25-inch map revision of 1913-14, with two horseshoe-type limekilns, close to housing. The quarry lay between a complex of railways and close to Kirkby Junction. Just to the east was a brick works, surrounded by houses.

Jack Rhodes, July 1930 [A5041] SK 503559

Limekilns at Portland Quarry, Mansfield Woodhouse, Nottinghamshire

The men are seen loading one of the limekilns, from a wagon loaded with Magnesian Limestone. The low kilns are stone-built with brick draw arches. They are of the flare type which are loaded, fired and allowed to cool before the burnt lime is removed. The process is then repeated. There is a good little tramway system at ground level, with six branches radiating from the turntable in the centre. The three wagons may contain burnt lime blocks. This scene is looking north, and photographs A5059-60 are general views of the same quarry. The quarry was worked by Harry Rouse, off Common Lane in Mansfield Woodhouse. Six men were here in 1931. Three limekilns are shown on the 25-inch map revision of 1914.

Jack Rhodes, August 1930 [A5061] SK 537635

Skegby Limeworks, Skegby, Nottinghamshire

The quarry is located immediately west of St Andrews church. The Lower Magnesian Limestone in this quarry is too thin-bedded and jointed to be of use for building, so it is really only suitable for limeburning. The picture shows the method of building a small 'horseshoe' limekiln, less sophisticated than those at Rouse's Portland Quarry. The kiln has been dug into a stone bed which provides a convenient loading platform. The front side walls are constructed of masonry, and the space between has been built up with bricks which will be removed so that the lime can be dug out once the burning is complete. The 25-inch map revision of 1914 shows five horseshoe limekilns in this quarry, and two old kilns in an adjoining disused quarry. Note also the small lorry. Painted on the side is: 'James Lees, Haulage Contractor, (1)44 Dalestorth St, Sutton Ashfield, Notts.' Lenicon Ltd was producing concrete products and limestone at the Old Skegby Lime Quarry, Woodhouse Lane, Skegby, in 1961-2.
Jack Rhodes, July 1930 [A5043] SK 491610

Dog Kennel Quarry and Lime Works, Kiveton, Yorkshire

Looking north-east, the quarry face displays well-bedded Lower Magnesian Limestone, below a good depth of soft overburden which is first dug and trammed away to the right. The limestone is unsuitable for building stone because of the close beds and joints, so it is being burnt for lime. There were five limekilns here; those on the right are banked up neatly in contrast to the ones at New Fryston. A rail-mounted steam crane on the top of the arched stone wall is used for loading the kilns behind. The second crane on the left is at right angles, giving access to the quarry face. There is a siding from the Sheffield to Worksop railway for carrying away the burnt lime. In 1931, 15 men were employed here by John W. Scaife & Sons Ltd, whose name is painted on the side of the railway wagon in the foreground. The firm also worked a quarry at Brancliffe, Shire Oaks.
Jack Rhodes, August 1930 [A5087] SK 508826

Kiveton Park Quarry, Yorkshire

Situated immediately to the west, but with less overburden than at Dog Kennel Quarry. Limeburning, however, is different. On the left is a rectangular Hoffman continuous kiln with a tall brick chimney. Note the incline for taking fuel to the top of the kiln. A lorry is parked at the lowest level for loading lime trammed straight from the kiln (photograph A5095 shows this in greater detail). The main structure in the centre of the photograph is a crushing and screening plant, with hoppers and chutes below. Electric power is supplied by cables seen on the right near the steam crane on rails. Concrete products were made here, such as the posts stacked on the ground. There are also piles of sawn blocks of stone brought from the nearby Anston Quarries in lorries, to be worked and 'masoned'. Both quarries were worked by James Turner & Son Ltd.

Jack Rhodes, Aug 1930 [A5090] SK 506826

Removing burnt lime from inside a kiln at Kiveton Park Quarry

This could not have been a very pleasant job as the men wear no protective gloves to load the burnt blocks of lime into iron-bodied wagons. The kiln chamber is brick-arched and the heavy glazing caused by firing can be seen in this photograph. The Hoffman kiln was a type designed for brickworks in 1857 but used for burning lime since 1864, the principal being that continuous burning is maintained by rotation through several chambers, with some being loaded while others are firing, cooling and discharging.

Jack Rhodes, August 1930 [A5094] SK 506826

New Fryston Quarry, near Castleford, Yorkshire

Three smoking limekilns can be seen in this view of the quarry, looking west. Note the construction of these 'horseshoe' kilns, partly excavated from the rock and with wedged poles apparently retaining their front walls of stone blocks. Planks across the gap to the kiln heads are for loading by wheelbarrows. They are 'flare kilns' which were loaded, fired and allowed to cool before discharge. An open or abandoned kiln can be seen on the left, while another is being dug out beyond the three working kilns. A similar kiln of this type is seen at Skegby in Nottinghamshire. Photograph A5203 shows a limekiln being built. The quarry was then worked by the Wheldale Lias Lime Co. The month is September, when some of the trees may have already lost their leaves - or have they been blighted? Whatever the case, the inhabitants of the lodge above the face would have got a poor deal. A contemporary map shows this as the Wheldale Wood Lias Lime Works with at least nineteen kilns, mostly in banks.

Jack Rhodes, September 1930 [A5201] SE 454267

Coxhoe Colliery Quarry, near Durham

Thin-bedded and jointed Lower Magnesian Limestone is being worked for dolomite. Looking north, the interest here is in the loading of a railway wagon painted 'S.L.Co.Ltd. No. 10.' The track has been cut down into the rock so the bedded limestone makes a loading platform at wagon top height. It is perhaps surprising that a quarry of this size should be still worked manually at this date, but the rock is so friable that the task can be done with relative ease. And labour was cheap. Coxhoe is 5 miles (8 km) south-east of Durham.

Jack Rhodes, September 1930 [A5252]
NZ 327363

Raisby Hill Quarries, near Durham

A view looking north-east, to show bedded dolomites of the lower Magnesian Limestone. Part of a railway siding can be seen, and one track tunnels through a narrow ridge (carrying a footpath through the quarries) to connect with workings beyond. The quarry, close to Coxhoe, was worked by the Raisby Hill Limestone Co. Ltd. at this date, and is still occupied by Raisby Quarries Ltd.

Jack Rhodes, September 1930 [A5250]
NZ 345352

CHAPTER NINE
LIMESTONE:
JURASSIC
PORTLAND STONE

THE MAIN JURASSIC LIMESTONES are found in a belt which extends from Portland and Purbeck on the south Dorset coast up through the Cotswolds and Lincolnshire to the Hambleton Hills of the North Yorkshire Moors. Many well known stones have been quarried along its length, and names such as Portland, Ham Hill, Doulting, Bath, Corsham, Guiting, Clipsham and Ancaster are all familiar to architects and builders (see Hudson, 1971). Quarries are still in operation in all these districts for new buildings and restoration work. The best freestones are oolitic limestones and have been used in prominent buildings throughout the country, including churches, cathedrals, public buildings and the universities at Oxford and Cambridge. The Lincolnshire Limestone (Inferior Oolite series) has produced a good building stone which can be seen in use in and around local villages. The best known quarries are at Ancaster (Lincolnshire) and Clipsham (Leicestershire). In Northamptonshire, Weldon Stone from the upper beds was quarried and worked underground. Great Weldon Quarry appears in a photograph [A8353] full of quarrying interest, but Jack Rhodes took it in 1949, too late to be included in this book. This limestone is seen in another context, in the nearby ironstone quarry at Longhills Pit. Tilestones and flags are other products from some limestone beds, as seen in the Cotswold

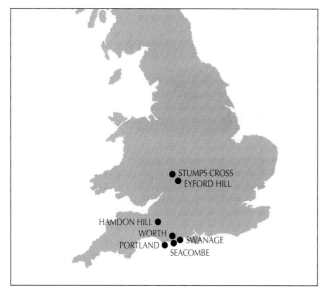

villages, or the so-called 'slates' of Stonesfield (Oxfordshire) and Collyweston (Northamptonshire).

The selected photographs are all of quarries in southern England. The first is from the Lower Jurassic in Somerset. Overlooking Norton and Stoke Sub Hamdon near Yeovil, Hamdon Hill has produced Ham Stone since Roman and Saxon times. Alec Clifton-Taylor called this rich golden freestone 'one of England's most seductive stones...' It is slightly oolitic, but coarsened with shell fragments and calcite, and is considered to represent the top of the Upper Lias. The stone was worked in small pits during the Middle Ages, when it was used for house and church building, as well as for tombs and other ornamental work. There was renewed activity in the sixteenth century, when stone was taken for neighbouring country houses such as Barrington Court and Montacute House. Quarries are still at work, and the Ham Hill Country Park has been established in the strange hummocky landscape created by centuries of activity on the hill top, which is itself enclosed by a vast iron age hillfort.

The Inferior Oolite of the Middle Jurassic is represented here by Stumps Cross Quarry in Gloucestershire. The Cotswold oolitic freestones were worked all the way south to Bath and beyond. The famous Bath Stone in the Great Oolite is unfortunately not in the BGS photographic collection.

From the Upper Jurassic are the Purbeck and Portland limestones of Dorset. Purbeck is an area known for its varied geology and related physical features. The famous Purbeck Marble, not a true marble but an attractive freshwater shelly limestone which takes a polish, was popular in the Middle Ages for altars, tombs, effigies as well as architectural stone for churches and cathedrals. However, in later years the many Purbeck limestone beds were quarried and mined for kerbs, channelling and building stone, while the underlying Purbeck-Portland freestones were worked for building stone from the coastal cliffs. Dorset's greatest Jurassic stone district is the Isle of Portland. The quarrying of Portland stone has been so concentrated on the island and is of such national importance that it is treated separately in this book.

Hamdon Hill Quarries, Somerset

This is a general view to the north, showing the Ham Stone in horizontal beds, cut in places by fissures. The workings in the foreground have been abandoned for some time, and activity is taking place in the background where a steam derrick lifts stone to the surface from a working bench part-way down the face. Note how the quarry opening has been backfilled with waste, held back by retaining walls. Up to 40 feet (12 metres) of overburden - sand and hardstone - might have to be removed. Blasting was necessary at times, and some hardstone used for stone tiles. All this effort was considered worthwhile, for the good Ham Stone extends down for a similar depth, with beds generally becoming thicker towards the bottom. The grey basement bed ('clout') is best for cornices and all weather courses in buildings.

Jack Rhodes, 11.15 a.m. April 1922 [A2157] ST 482162

Hamdon Hill stone works

A stone cutting machine, used to prepare stone for planing. Note the narrow vertical saw blade and the saw pit below. The flat block of stone is placed on a travelling bed which can be moved slowing past the reciprocating saw blade. A piece has been sawn off and the second cut is about to start, the block having been firmly wedged in position. The building behind can still be identified at the Norton Masonry Works where quarrying and stone dressing are still undertaken.

Jack Rhodes, 11 a.m. April 1922 [A2156]
ST 482163

67

Quarrying at Hamdon Hill

The traditional method of quarrying at Hamdon Hill. This is a rare photograph showing two quarrymen at work, using picks to cut out a deep groove along the joint planes wherever possible. Blocks of stone will then be detached by wedges driven horizontally along a bedding plane and levered out with bars. The distinctive marks left behind by this age-old method can still be seen in the faces of abandoned quarries. The Ham Hill & Doulting Stone Co. Ltd. was the main firm on the hill, having taken over from the Ham Hill Stone Co. in 1896. In 1920, the firm employed 51 men here.

Jack Rhodes, 12.50 p.m. April 1922 [A2161] ST 482162

Stumps Cross Quarry, near Stanway, Gloucestershire

This shallow quarry, 3$\frac{1}{2}$ miles (5.6 km) east-north-east of Winchcombe, is yielding 'Yellow Guiting Stone', a freestone from the Inferior Oolite. Good-sized blocks for building have been trimmed and are waiting beside the timber hand-derrick. Note the long bar leaning against the quarry face next to the worker standing on the right. Compare this with the bar seen at Linby Quarry, Nottinghamshire. This and the following photograph have been published by the Geological Survey (Richardson, 1929).

Jack Rhodes, April 1928 [A4232] SP 078302

Tilestones at Eyford Hill, Gloucestershire

Tilestones or Cotswold slates are stacked ready for transport near the Cotswold Slate Co's shallow Eyford Hill pit, 3½ miles (5.6 km) west of Stow-on-the-Wold. Slates from here were used for roofing locally and as far away as the Oxford colleges. The fissile stones were laid out like a mosaic carpet across the fields during the winter for 'frosting' (shown in BGS photograph A4248). It was important for the stone to retain 'sap' and water so it could be split by the action of the frost. This was a technique employed at similar places such as Stonesfield in Oxfordshire and Collyweston in Northamptonshire, where the stone was mined at both sites. Once split, the stones would be trimmed to shape and a hole cut for fixing. Slates were also made near Eyford Hill at Huntsman's Quarry where the cost of production was reduced by selling stone from a crushing plant. Note the Cotswold drystone wall with irregular heavy copestones ('combers') in the foreground.

Jack Rhodes, April 1928 [A4249] ?SP 135255

Raising a stone block in Seacombe Quarry, Dorset

A 4½-ton block is being lifted by a pair of 'dogs'. When attached to a crane's chain sling, these heavy blunt hooks pinch in and grip the stone as it is lifted, obviating the difficult procedure of somehow first raising a heavy block to place a lifting chain beneath it. This is a large block from the Purbeck-Portland beds, which are far more broken than in the Portland quarries. Compressed air drills made vertical holes for inserting wedges for dislodging blocks from their beds (shown in BGS photograph A4982).

Jack Rhodes, April 1930 [A4985] SY 984766

Seacombe Quarry, near Worth Matravers, Dorset

The Purbeck-Portland beds are of a slightly different and tougher character than those on Portland, and are exposed along the 5-mile (8 km) stretch of coast westwards from Durlston Head near Swanage. They were worked here in cliff-side quarries which continued underground in many places. The view is looking north-west, with the sea on the left behind the crane, dressing shed and compressor house. The larger of the two timber hand-derricks has the thickened mast base so typical of the Portland cranes. A steam derrick with a lattice steel jib is working higher up the cliff in the background. Note also the pipes for distributing compressed air to drills at the working faces from the plant behind the workshed. Entrances to underground workings can be seen at the foot of the face on the right. Stone from most cliff quarries was traditionally lowered into barges, but Seacombe had the advantage of inland access down a steep valley. The quarry was being worked at this date by the Dorset Quarry Co. Ltd., employing 34 men. Now closed, it is still a site familiar to walkers along the Dorset Coastal Footpath.

Jack Rhodes, April 1930 [A4958] SY 984766

Underground at Seacombe Quarry

Seacombe was also worked underground, as at Winspit, Dancing Ledge, Tilly Whim and other Purbeck coastal quarries. This view shows how the roof is supported here by 'legs' of drystone blocks and some rather narrow pillars of uncut Purbeck-Portland stone. While enabling more stone to be extracted, this was less secure than leaving broader pillars, as used in other parts of the Seacombe and cliffside quarries. The 'house cap' forms a good roof and the working method is to first remove the thin 'underpicking' layer beneath it, to gain access to the top of the commercial stone which is then removed. A compressed air pipe leading to the working area can be seen alongside the righthand tramway rail.

Jack Rhodes, April 1930 [A4962] SY 984766

Worth Quarries, near Worth Matravers, Dorset

An expanding quarry operation, working the Purbeck-Portland beds on the Isle of Purbeck. Much of the stone is too fractured to be of use for buildings, so it is crushed for roadstone or burnt for lime. The stone is being quarried by hand, making use of the natural horizontal beds to work it in benches. The face is being cleared methodically in a tidy manner, with broken stone stacked neatly ready to be carried away in the skips on the small tramway. There is a slight gradient and motive power is supplied by the petrol-engined Simplex-type locomotive seen here. Note the section of Jubilee track and the older type of tipping skip on the left. The mixed-feed limekiln is a vertical steel cylinder lined with Stourbridge firebricks. Limestone and culm are loaded at the top by skips drawn up the incline on the right. Note also the tall crushing and screening plant beyond. A second, larger, kiln was added soon after this photograph; both survived until the end of the decade. Worth Quarries Ltd employed 48 men here in 1930 but was taken over by Swanworth Quarries Ltd three years later. The quarry, now much enlarged, is still worked for roadstone.

Jack Rhodes, April 1930 [A5018] SY 969784

Purbeck stone mine, near Swanage, Dorset

Purbeck limestone beds were worked at the surface in open quarries and underground 'quarrs' on the hills above and to the west of Swanage. These narrow beds of tough stone were sought for kerbs and paving, which found a ready market in London, to which they were shipped from Swanage until the opening of the railway in 1885. It is hard to believe that the seafront of this popular resort was once no better than a masons' yard. John Mowlem (1788-1868), founder of the great construction company, was a Swanage man who built up his reputation in this trade in the mid-nineteenth century. The stone is still worked today, opencast, and several of the beds take a polish making an attractive ornamental stone, with names such as Thornback, Whitstone, White Horse, Dun Cow, Rag and Roach.

This view shows the entrance to an inland 'quarr' or stone mine, looking north. A horse is attached to the 'spack' pole, and walks around a circle to turn the capstan which is set between two upright 'crab-stones'. A chain hauls up the heavily-constructed 'quarr cart' or 'trundle' which runs on grooves (not rails) cut in the stone of the inclined shaft. The spack was usually of ash, and the capstan of elm with an oak collar. In 1911, there were 51 mines, employing 91 men below and 60 men above ground. They were all small family undertakings, usually worked by two or three men each. Most Purbeck mines were named after their owners, such as 'Fred Bower's' or 'F. Seymour's.' The working conditions of these mines and the social life of the quarrymen have been described by Eric Benfield (1990).

Jack Rhodes, 11.15 a.m. 17 October 1911 [A1303] ? SZ 0278

Purbeck stone mine at Cowleaze, Swanage, Dorset

This must be a nearby mine, as it was photographed just half an hour later. The shaft comes up and enters the door in the wall to reach the capstan. Note the drystone wall and sheds with Purbeck stone tile roofs which enclose the sheltered working area at the top of the shaft. This hillside at Cowleaze above Swanage was riddled with similar workings. Two other mines can be seen here; one behind this mine is identified by the stack of finished kerbs on the left, and the other is down near the terraced cottages to the right. The town of Swanage was expanding at this time and streets can be seen laid out in the fields behind the bay prior to house building.

Jack Rhodes, 11.45 a.m. 17 October 1911 [A1304] SZ 024784

PORTLAND STONE

Some of the most famous quarries in England were developed on the Isle of Portland, a 4-mile (6.4 km) bastion of stone projecting into the English Channel and held to the mainland only by Chesil Beach. Portland's plateau-top dips gently from around 480 feet (146 metres) in the north to sea level at Portland Bill. Portland stone was used outside the island in the Roman and medieval periods, but its main fortunes date from the early seventeenth century onwards. Although Inigo Jones chose it for the Banqueting Hall in Whitehall, Portland stone is most closely associated with Sir Christopher Wren who took thousands of tons for rebuilding St Paul's Cathedral and other London churches after the Great Fire of 1666. Supplies were seemingly unlimited, but more significant was the quality of this attractive white freestone, which could resist the ravages of a polluted city atmosphere more than other limestones.

The development of markets in London, especially for public buildings, was aided by the coastal location of Portland, despite the difficulties of getting the stone down from the quarries to the various shipping places. Transport was much improved by the Merchants' Railway (1826-1939) which brought stone down a long incline to Castletown Pier in Portland Harbour. This had a gauge of 4 feet 6 inches (1.37 metres) and there were numerous branches into the quarries on the top of Portland. The Admiralty, or Breakwater Railway served the breakwater construction works which began in 1849. Although there had been a branch from the main line at Weymouth since 1865, the standard gauge Easton & Church Hope Railway was not opened onto the top of the island until 1900. Thus, for the first time stone could be sent direct from the central quarries and masonry yards to inland destinations throughout mainland Britain.

The first two photographs were taken by Jack Rhodes in 1912, when there were 560 men employed in 33 quarries on Portland. There had been more than twice that number a

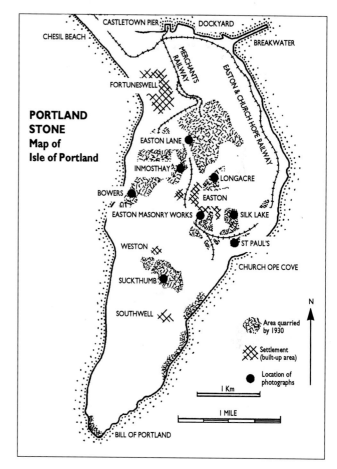

PORTLAND STONE
Map of Isle of Portland

decade before, when the Portland Breakwater extensions were being carried out. The two largest firms in 1912 were the Bath Stone Firms Ltd and F. J. Barnes, who employed 68 per cent of the quarrymen. Trade recovered well after the effects of the Great War, with a major part being in war memorials and headstones for the War Graves Commission. An employment peak was reached in 1931 (a year after the main photographs here), with 905 men in 43 quarry workings. The Bath & Portland Stone Firms Ltd (renamed since 1911) and F. J. Barnes now had a greater share of the workforce. Two other important firms were the South Western Stone Co. (previously the United Stone Firms Ltd) and John Pearce Portland Stone Co. Ltd. The larger Bath & Portland group took over F. J. Barnes three years later, and the South Western Stone Co. in 1960 (see Bezzant, 1980). Still active on Portland, the Bath & Portland Stone Ltd is itself a subsidiary of ARC.

A large part of Portland has been turned over for stone, with some quarries at the top (north) end of the island requiring the removal of 40 feet (12 metres) of overlying Purbeck beds of thin limestones and shales. The hard Cap must be blasted before reaching the three main Portland beds of commercial value. The first is the Roach, a tough shelly stone useful for civil engineering, and below this are the prized freestones named the Whitbed (the true Portland stone) and the Basebed. Traditional quarrying methods on Portland were described by Smeaton (1791) and updated by Wallis (1891) and Hounsell (1952).

Stone quarry at Easton, looking north-east

An early photograph in the series, showing a quiet corner of an unnamed quarry. The typical Portland type of timber hand-derrick has a thickened base to the mast and one supporting stay anchored firmly atop massive waste blocks. Blocks of up to 12 tons were said to have been discarded, and the size of the ones here seem to confirm this. Note the blocks of Whitbed squared or 'scappled' with 'kivels', the tool marks of which are clearly seen. The damaged block in the left foreground has three quarrymen's marks: the carved 'P' within a diamond was the mark of the quarrier F. J. Barnes, and the location could therefore be Barnes' Inmosthay East or West Quarries, which had sidings just north-north-west of Easton. The stone-laden wagon is on a branch of the horse-drawn Merchants' Railway. There appears to be a tunnel cut through the unquarried rock behind.

Jack Rhodes, June 1912
[A1419] ?SY 689725

74

Longacre Quarry

Another good early photograph. A gang of six men is having lunch beside a strong timber hand-derrick of 10 tons capacity. The quarry is being working towards the camera, and the ladder in front of the men indicates the position of the very narrow face. Note also the squared blocks and the neatly built drystone retaining wall for the quarry waste on the left. Five other derricks can be seen in this quarry, with others beyond on the horizon. 'Bath Stone Firms Ltd' is painted on one crane's jib. Rhodes gave the orientation of this photograph as east-south-east, but it is more likely to be west-south-west if it is indeed Longacre Quarry. A 'quarry jack' is propped against the foot of the jib of the nearest crane. Although crab-winches with shear legs had been in use, hand-cranes were not introduced to Portland until about 1850; steam cranes came after 1893.

Jack Rhodes, 12.10 p.m. June 1912 [A1422] SY 695722

Quarry jack at Bowers Quarry

Lifting jacks were a traditional Portland method of raising stone blocks in the quarries. This one is still in use in 1930.

Jack Rhodes, April 1930 [A4972]

Suckthumb Quarry

This informative overall scene looking east shows the depth and nature of the overlying Purbeck strata, rubble and cap above the building stone. The very narrow working 'gullet' is clearly seen in this photograph. All the while, the advancing quarry face cuts into the Portland fields, to leave a huge area of disturbed ground where the overburden has been tipped behind strong benches of waste blocks built at different levels. On the lower bench in the foreground a gang of three men is dealing with a block beneath the crane's hook, while the crane-driver waits in attendance. Note the 'ladder' up the stays of the crane, giving access for maintenance. There are two other steam derricks, and the distant one has a lattice steel jib. Quarrymen's huts could be moved to where they were needed, and the one in the foreground has a wire sling around it for this purpose. The small timber hand-derrick on the left is remarkably similar to a 3-ton crane which stood in this quarry until about 1990, when the old workings were infilled with waste. Roadways approach the cranes through gaps in the upper bench, allowing wagons - still drawn by traction engines at this date - to be loaded with blocks. Note picks and kivels by the crane's stay in the foreground. Photograph A4976, looking west from this point, shows a fourth steam crane lifting waste to a skip tramway on a high bench. In 1931, F. J. Barnes had 106 men working at Suckthumb. Another section of this extensive quarry was owned, but not being worked, by the Bath & Portland Stone Firms Ltd.

Jack Rhodes, April 1930 [A4952] SY 687706

Silklake Quarry

An army of cranes appears to be advancing across Portland's ancient strip fields or 'lawnsheds', the divisions of which are identified by low earthen baulks. Five large lattice steel steam cranes are in action, two with flying jibs which enable waste to be deposited on top of the unusually high benches behind. The distant crane is landing a rubble skip. The jib of the second crane bears the plate: 'John A. Sangster 15 tons Aberdeen.' Because the quarry face is hidden between the cranes and the fields, the working area must be extremely narrow. Silklake Quarry was first opened up in 1912. The quarrier A. G. Coombe was employing 33 men in three sections of the quarry by 1931. The view is looking north-west, and the cranes in the far distance are working in the Broadcroft Quarries, an extension of the Longacre Quarry seen above.

Jack Rhodes, April 1930 [A4974] SY 698717

Steam channeller at Bowers Quarry

A steam channeller at work, making cuts of about 4 feet (1.2 metres) deep. The quarrymen usually made use of natural joints, but sometimes straight lines were needed, such as when they were working right up to the boundary of a property. The machine has a vertical boiler and is mounted on rails strengthened with diagonal cross-bracing. The cutting blade and the resulting channel can be seen on the right. The machine seen at the Storeton sandstone quarry in Cheshire is similar but has a horizontal boiler. Channellers were not the norm on Portland, although it is recorded that Anderson & Son had supplied a second-hand machine to the Bath Stone Firms Ltd here much earlier in about 1900 (Bezzant, 1980, 184). The distinctive faces left behind by channellers are still seen in some abandoned coastal quarries to the north-east of Portland Bill.

Jack Rhodes, April 1930 [A4981] ?SY 682719

Splitting a block at St Paul's Quarry

Using scales and wedges to split a block of Portland stone. A shallow groove has first been 'pitted' with a 'twabill', the pick which can be seen lying on the stone (this operation is shown in photograph A4986). Wedges are then placed between thin iron or steel strips ('scales') and struck in line with sledge hammers. Note the three timber derricks in the background, and, on the extreme left, the arched entrance of the medieval Rufus Castle which stands on a high rock commanding the old landing beach at Church Ope Cove on the east coast. This quarry was being worked by the Bath & Portland Stone Firms Ltd at the time of the photograph.

Jack Rhodes, April 1930 [A4987] SY 698713

Transporting blocks of Portland stone at Easton

Two trailer-wagons are being hauled by a Burrel traction engine of the Bath & Portland Stone Firms Ltd. The firm had owned traction engines since 1913, but they were replaced a year after this photograph by a fleet of Sentinel steam lorries. The load is stopped on Easton Lane (now Easton Road), 'going to the railway' which would be at Priory Corner where a crane still transferred stone onto the Merchants' Railway. These large blocks give a good idea of the size of stone obtained from the quarries. Note the marks painted on them, giving details such as the source quarry, quarry gang, cubic size and stock number.

Jack Rhodes, April 1930 [A4995] SY 690728

The works of the Bath & Portland Stone Firms Ltd at Easton

Looking north-east into the Bottomcombe Masonry Works at Easton, bought by the firm in 1904 from the Easton Stone Saw Mills Co (Webber & Pangbourne Ltd). The place was modernised in the 1920s, with the addition of new cutting machines and saw frames, powered by an oil engine and generator, and a new steel overhead gantry with travelling cranes. The workyard was extended further and converted to electricity a year after this photograph was taken. Having been brought here from the quarries, rough blocks are first shaped by frame saws on the right; note the stacks of sawn and partly sawn blocks. The masonry department is behind and to the left. Two 5-ton overhead electric travelling cranes, built by Sir William Arrol & Co. Ltd of Glasgow in 1925, handle stones in the yard. Finished stones, and also quarried blocks, were despatched inland by rail via the Easton and Church Hope Railway, from which there was a direct siding into the workyard. The railway wagons seen here belong to the four main railway companies, suggesting widely dispersed destinations for the stone. Note the LNER container carried on another wagon.

Jack Rhodes, April 1930 [A4997] SY692716

Frame saws at Easton

Three workmen pose in front of a frame saw which works with a reciprocating action. Steel plates move back and forth across a stone block, the cutting action being aided by sharp sand added to the sawn groove. A second machine on the right has a large block sawn into thick slabs.

Jack Rhodes, April 1930 [A4998] SY692716

Coulter planing machine at the Easton Masonry Works

The machine (Coulter & Harpin's Patent No. 379) works by passing chisels across the stone, gouging out a measured depth each time.

Jack Rhodes, April 1930 [A5004] SY692716

Rubbing a stone at the Easton works

The stone is being rubbed with a block to put on a final face, having first been scratched with steel combs set in a wood block (a process illustrated in photograph A5005).

Jack Rhodes, April 1930 [A5006] SY692716

Masons' workshop at Easton

The men are absent, but we can see their work in this busy workshop. There are sections of fluted shafts and, centre foreground, an upended capital being shaped out. Note the masons' mallets and other tools, the small overhead crane, and the main power shaft with a line of pulleys and belt drives for machinery.

Jack Rhodes, April 1930 [A5008] SY692716

CHAPTER TEN
ROADSTONE & AGGREGATES

ROADSTONE REPRESENTS BY FAR the most common type of quarry worked in the twentieth century, and the term embraces crushed and graded stones sought for road-making, railway ballast, or aggregates for concrete. Today, the production of aggregates (including sand and gravel) far outstrips all other stone types. Output rose steadily throughout the twentieth century, with a dramatic increase in the 1960s so that today the annual output is around 300 million tonnes for the United Kingdom. Quarries, ranging in size from small roadside pits to massive mechanised operations, have been opened in suitable hard rocks wherever there are nearby markets or good transport facilities. These include igneous rocks of basalt, diorite, gabbro, granite and syenite which are mostly found in the upland and western districts of England and Wales. Elsewhere, small outcrops of granodiorites have been exploited for roadstone and street setts around Mountsorrel in Leicestershire, and there are the basalts, diorites and metamorphic quartzites of the Staffordshire and Warwickshire quarries which are described below. Their location in the heart of the English Midlands makes these exposures particularly valuable. Major roadstone quarries are found in the Carboniferous limestones of the Derbyshire and Yorkshire Pennines, the Mendip Hills of Somerset and in South Wales. Hard sandstones and gritstones are also worked,

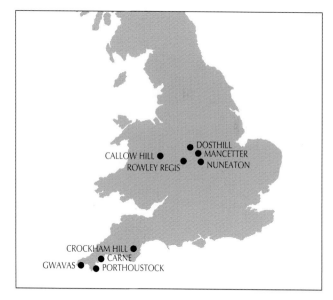

while building stone quarries may produce some crushed stone as a useful by-product and a means of disposing of unwanted waste.

The photographs include roadstone quarries in Cornwall, Devon, Shropshire, Staffordshire and Warwickshire. Cornwall has many hard igneous rocks, among them dykes of quartz porphyry, locally called elvan. Roadstone quarrying developed from the late nineteenth century onwards, but local markets for stone are limited. As a result, the larger roadstone quarries were opened on the coast, allowing their products to be shipped off as far as London and northern European ports. Such quarries were developed at Penlee in Mount's Bay, around Porthoustock on the Lizard and at Stepper Point near Padstow on the north coast. Smaller quarries were worked beside the River Lynher, a branch of the Tamar estuary, by which barges carried the stone to Plymouth. Similar igneous roadstone quarries were also located along the Welsh coasts, such as at Penmaenmawr or Trevor in Caernarvonshire (Gwynedd), and Porthgain in Pembrokeshire (Dyfed).

In Devon, quarries were opened up in dolerite around Trusham in the Teign valley, taking advantage of the presence of a railway. The largest igneous roadstone quarry today is on the northern flank of Dartmoor at Meldon near Okehampton, worked in dolerite and still retaining a rail link to Exeter. Limestones and gritstones are also sources of roadstone in the county.

Shropshire has yielded roadstones and aggregates from a variety of rocks. The Clee Hill dhustone is a fine-grained olivine-dolerite which makes a roadstone of national fame, and its quarries were once served by a branch railway and inclines. The Silurian Wenlock limestones around Much Wenlock, have been quarried for roadstone, as well as for building, smelting flux and lime. Cambrian and Ordovician quartzites have been quarried around the Wrekin and Stiperstones.

In the Midlands, the Nuneaton inlier (Warwickshire) is a narrow belt of ancient Cambrian rocks, about 9 miles (14 kilometres) long and 1 mile (1.6 kilometre) wide. It includes the pale pinkish-grey Hartshill Quartzites and intrusive diorites suitable for roadstone. The early success of all these quarries was dependent on the use of canal and rail transport. It was no exaggeration when a trade directory commented of Hartshill: 'Tramways have been laid down to the North Western main line and to the canal navigation, and afford unusual facilities for mineral transport' (Kelly, 1912, 133). Other quarries were developed in igneous rocks at Dosthill and Rowley Regis in neighbouring Staffordshire, and they too made some use of canals and railways.

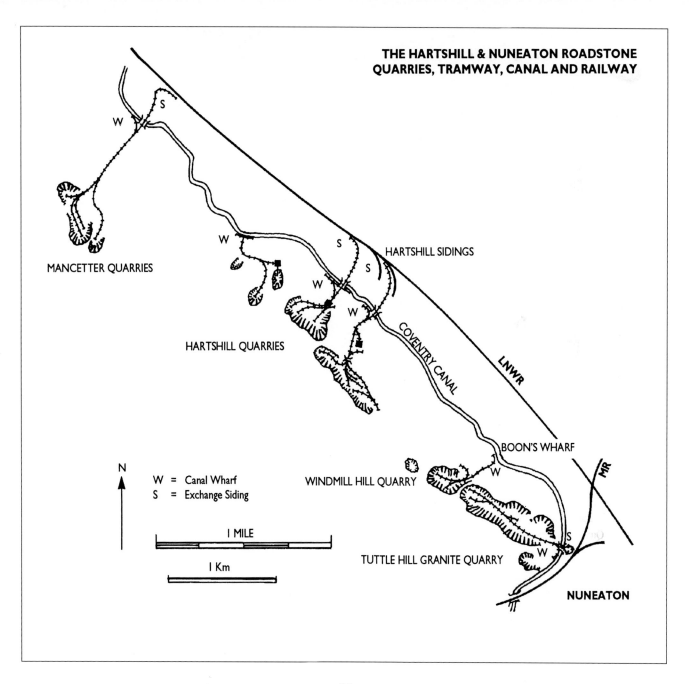

THE HARTSHILL & NUNEATON ROADSTONE
QUARRIES, TRAMWAY, CANAL AND RAILWAY

MANCETTER QUARRIES

HARTSHILL SIDINGS

HARTSHILL QUARRIES

COVENTRY CANAL

LNWR

BOON'S WHARF

MIR

WINDMILL HILL QUARRY

N

W = Canal Wharf
S = Exchange Siding

1 MILE

1 Km

TUTTLE HILL GRANITE QUARRY

NUNEATON

Carne Quarry, Veryan, Cornwall

A small rural quarry of the early twentieth century, this one in a local exposure of Ordovician quartzite between Veryan and Nare Head in the Roseland peninsula of the south Cornish coast. Surface outcrops can be seen at the top of the quarry face. Said to produce an excellent roadstone, it was difficult to quarry by hand - bars, sledgehammers and shovels are among the tools visible. The more jointed stone has been worked away to form an overhanging face on the right. There is no evidence of blasting although this was probably necessary to dislodge the larger blocks. Note the lad patiently tending the horse and cart, indicating the small quantities of stone which were carried away with each load. John Reynolds was recorded as the quarry owner intermittently between 1910 and 1922. Is he perhaps the boatered gentleman seen standing with a dog? There is a second dog between the two quarrymen, so this was almost literally a 'one man and his dog' operation.

T.C. Hall, 11 a.m. 27 May 1905 [A143] ?SW 9138

Porthoustock Quarry jetty, Lizard peninsula, Cornwall

At the turn of the century, roadstone quarries were developed in outcrops of gabbro, hornblende schist and epidiorite (blue elvan) along the cliffs around Porthoustock Cove on the east coast of the Lizard peninsula. The problems of transport and marketing were solved by building jetties from which coasters could be loaded with roadstone. Despite appearances, this jetty on the north side of the cove was newly built, but was later modified considerably. Note the older-style tramway wagons bringing stone from the quarries to the top of the precarious high level bridge, from the end of which stone is tipped down a long loading chute which can be raised or lowered according to the state of tide. Lesser chutes at the sides and a tramway at an intermediate level feed the storage bins below. Skip wagons on the quay receive stone from the bins for tipping into ships alongside. The cove is exposed to the east, so it was necessary to stockpile a good quantity of stone to load ships without delay. Sailing vessels, steamers and, later, motor coasters all called here. The St Keverne Stone Co. began quarrying in about 1896, and was employing 83 men when this photograph was taken in 1908. The firm became the Porthoustock & St Keverne Stone Co. in the following year. The quarries closed in the 1960s, but the jetty still remains. Across the cove, the Rosenython Quarry worked from 1906 until 1975, and BGS photograph A655 shows its loading jetty and the still very small quarry in 1908. The beach in Porthoustock Cove has been extended seawards over the years as a result of quarry waste being thrown into the sea (Bird, 1987, 83-92).

T.C. Hall, 1.10 p.m. 20 July 1908 [A656] SW 808219

Gwavas Quarry, Newlyn, Cornwall

A photograph full of detail, showing the stone crushing and screening plant at a quarry in a tough altered dolerite. Quarried stone is trammed to the top and fed from a charging platform into the stone-breaker which is bolted down to a concrete platform and driven with a belt from a portable steam engine. Cast on the machine is 'R BROADBENT & SON LTD MAKERS STALYBRIDGE PATENT IMPROVED BLAKE STONE BREAKER' - compare this with the advertisement reproduced on page 10. The crushed stone passes through the revolving screen, a perforated drum which grades the product according to size, and then falls through chutes into the waiting skip wagons. BGS photograph A273 shows tramways at the main quarry workings on the far side of the arch seen in this view. An existing track crossed the tramway on the arch and then continued along a narrow causeway of unquarried ground. The roadstone was stockpiled or sent direct by a 2 foot (60cm) gauge tramway beside the shore to Newlyn's South Pier, where there were facilities for loading coasters. The German-built steam locomotive 'Penlee' hauled wagons along this line from about 1900 until the 1940s. This railway was replaced by a conveyor belt in 1972. At the time of the photograph, the quarry was being worked by the newly formed Penlee & St Ives Stone Quarries Ltd who employed 77 men at this and the adjacent Penlee Quarry. As elsewhere in the quarry industry, activity fluctuated dramatically according to demand, for the workforce had been 119 men in the previous year. The two early workings have long since combined and the huge Penlee Quarry has expanded back into the hillside and towards Newlyn from this original site opposite Carn Gwavas. The quarry produced an aggregate with a crushing strength said to be higher than any other in Britain, but has now closed.

T.C. Hall, 2 p.m. 24 April 1906 [A274]
SW 469278

Crockham Hill Quarry, near Chudleigh, Devon

Roadstone quarrying was developed here after 1905 by the Teign Valley Granite Co. At the time of this photograph just three years later, 96 men were employed. Operations would not have been successful without a siding from the Teign Valley Railway, a branch opened from Heathfield near Chudleigh Knighton to Ashton in 1882, and extended to Exeter in 1903. This rather distant view, looking north-west, shows an example of a quarry face being excavated in a dolerite intrusion forming a valleyside spur, with men working on a low level bench. On the left is the crushing and screening plant, with small hoppers for loading railway wagons on the quarry siding. On the railway in the foreground is an assortment of Great Western Railway wagons, with the two on the right owned by the Teign Valley Granite Co. After 1934, the quarry was worked by Roads Reconstruction Ltd. Later specialising in the manufacture of pre-cast concrete pipes and other products, it was this traffic that kept the last section of the railway from Heathfield open until the 1960s. Today, ARC Southern make concrete products here, but the scene is barely recognisable because much of the hillside behind has been lost to the renamed Trusham Quarry. Hall recorded this view as Trusham Quarry, but in his time that particular quarry was across the valley (out of the picture to the right).

T.C. Hall, 9.15 a.m. 5 June 1908 [A538] SX 849809

Callow Hill Quarry, near Minsterley, Shropshire

This is a good picture of a small rural roadstone quarry, worked in the Ordovician Mytton Group of siltstones, with a dolerite dyke visible on the right. Some 23 years after the Carne Quarry photograph, quarrying here is seen to be more organised. Men are loading a side-tipping skip wagon on a small tramway which leads, presumably, to a crusher. The fixed tramway in the foreground is laid with heavier rails, but the two branches to the face are temporary as they need to be moved to wherever quarrying is taking place. Note the crude point system, by which one rail is lifted across manually. A section of Jubilee track is discarded on the left. The view is looking east and joints in the rock show up well in the face. This quarry was being worked at this date by Haywards Quarries Ltd, who also owned a large quarry at Nills Hill (Pontesbury), and others at Grimmer (Minsterley), Crows Nest (Snailbeach) and Upper Mill (Bishop's Castle). Callow Hill has since grown out of all proportions, later worked by Shropshire County Council and more recently by Tarmac Roadstone (Western) Ltd.

Jack Rhodes, July 1929 [A4799] SJ 386050

Windmill Quarry, Tuttle Hill, near Nuneaton, Warwickshire

A roadstone quarry worked in the Park Hill Quartzite. The steeply dipping beds of the Middle or Tuttle Hill Quartzite are seen in the upper part on the left, in this view which looks north-west. Jack Rhodes was up early to take this photograph, and the quarrymen are already at work on the face below the windmill, no doubt taking advantage of the long summer day. Note the tramways and the wagons on three different levels. The windmill above the quarry is believed to have been the last windmill in the country to have been fitted with five sails, this following an accident. The tower remains today. The building on the left is Camp Hill Farm. The quarriers, William Boon & Sons, employed 35 men at this date. Being restricted by the windmill and a main road on the left, the quarry face has advanced only a short distance further since the photograph. However, it has been greatly deepened and incorporated into the neighbouring Tuttle Hill Granite Quarry (Judkins Ltd) which expanded from the east. In 1994, Windmill Quarry was still being worked by ARC, but the eastern end was being backfilled with refuse.
Jack Rhodes, 7.20 a.m. 12 June 1913 [A1621] SP 343932

Jee's washing and loading plant near the Anchor Inn, Hartshill, near Nuneaton

The washing plant is for freeing the quartzite from thin shale partings, the dirt being collected in mud pits and sludge beds beyond this view. The bucket lift and the revolving screen or trommel at the top of the plant are worked by the steam engine mounted on a raised brick and concrete platform. Note also the chutes for loading narrow boats on the Coventry Canal and the rail-mounted steam crane beyond. The quarry company possessed six barges or narrow boats for transporting roadstone, or larger blocks which had to be loaded more carefully. Of the latter, some went as far as Banbury Union workhouse via the Grand Union Canal. Quarried stone was also sent on a tramway across the canal bridge behind to a siding beside the London & North Western Railway. The quarriers later owned over 70 railway wagons for use on the main line. The wharf and engine platform can be still identified today, with the quarry offices now built upon them. The tramway bridge and the Anchor Inn (behind the camera, and seen in the next plate) also survive.
Jack Rhodes, 12 noon, 16 June 1913 [A1626] SP 336946

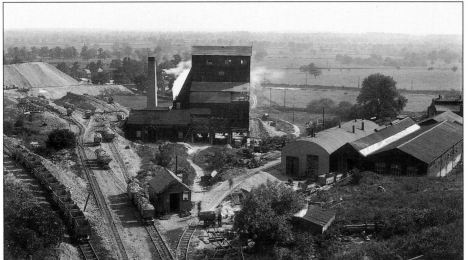

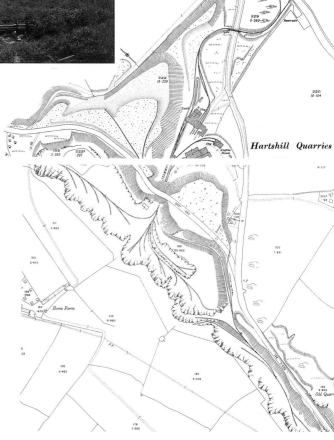

Hartshill Quarries

Jee's Quarry, Hartshill, near Nuneaton, Warwickshire

Looking north-east down and over the main steam-powered crushing and screening plant, this view was taken from a bridge carrying a lane which traversed the quarry workings. Stone from the Lower and Middle Quartzite is brought on the tramways from the quarry which lies behind the camera position. Most wagons are square timber-sided and side-tipping, but a few Jubilee skips can be seen. The beaten path between the rails of the two main tracks indicates the wagon trains were horse-drawn, although here the individual wagons were pushed by hand. Later, the quarry company possessed six steam locomotives. Six loaded wagons are stopped at the weighbridge beside the attendant weighbridge house, before moving on to be tipped into the crushing plant. Three tracks allow wagons to be loaded from the hoppers beneath the tall screening plant. From here a tramway curves away first to the left and then to the right, crossing a road, to the washing and canalside loading plant which is just visible through the steam between the square chimney stack and screening building. A branch (hidden by the screening plant) continued across the canal to the main line railway. The Anchor Inn and a road bridge over the canal are visible between the chimney and waste tip on the left. The repair shops are in the long buildings on the right, with an engine house beyond. Some work is going on near the weighbridge house in the centre foreground, where a side-tipping wagon stands at the end of a temporary inclined track laid over the line to the workshops. Jee's Hartshill Granite & Brick Co. Ltd employed 130 men here in 1913. Renamed the Nuneaton Quarry, it was being worked by Tarmac Roadstone Ltd in 1994.

Jack Rhodes, June 1913 [A1624] SP 335944

Mancetter Quarries, Purley Chase, near Oldbury, Warwickshire

A diorite quarry, some 2 miles (3.2 kilometres) north-west of Jee's Quarry, although still within the Nuneaton Cambrian rocks. In 1913, the quarries were being worked by William Linney Ireland, who employed 88 men. The photograph looks south-west and gives a view of the crushing and screening plant, but the purpose-built tramway wagons are the main interest. The figure leans against a line of seven side-tipping wagons containing different grades of stone, braked with a short length of rail jammed through a wheel of the first wagon. Heaps of waste form hills in the background, beyond which the quarry itself was being worked in a restricted area almost up to the Oldbury reservoir of the Coventry Canal. As at Jee's Quarry, the tramway took stone to the canal and main line railway, the route passing out of this picture to the left.
Jack Rhodes, 3.10 p.m. 14 June 1913 [A1640] SP 310957

Dosthill Granite Quarry, near Tamworth, Staffordshire

A view looking down into this roadstone quarry, 2½ miles (4 kilometres) south of Tamworth. Three laden stone wagons wait to be hauled to the surface from the bottom of a double incline, from which many tracks radiate to the various working faces, an arrangement typical of this type of quarry. The wagons are all open on one side to aid loading (and discharge) by hand - there are no cranes or excavators. The incline is hauled by a continuous cable, the lower sheave wheel, or return pulley, is beneath the boarding underneath the two wagons. Note the vertical boiler of the steam plant which is more permanent than the one seen at Prospect Quarry. A steam pipe leads away beneath two tramway tracks to a rock-drill at the face. The so-called 'granite' of this quarry is part of the Dosthill inlier of Cambrian age, which is intruded by sills of dark green hornblendic rocks. The Dosthill Granite Quarry Co. Ltd. employed 46 men here in 1913. The Ordnance Survey 1:2500 maps of 1921 show a stone crusher positioned at the top of the incline, from which there were two aerial cableways. One ran east-south-east for 875 yards (800 metres) to a loading point at the Dosthill Granite Sidings from the Midland Railway (Birmingham and Derby), while the other cableway ran west-south-west across the River Tame to the Birmingham and Fazely Canal. The quarry is now disused and flooded.
Jack Rhodes, 1.40 p.m. 15 October 1912 [A1531] SP 211998

Rock-drill at Prospect Quarry

Three weighted legs hold this steam rock drill firmly while drilling near-horizontal holes in preparation for blasting. Note the star-shaped drill bit, the steam pipe, and the spanners and other tools propped against the face. On either side of the tools are two drilled holes which have been plugged with paper to keep them dry and are ready to receive an explosive charge. Photograph A9145 is a general view showing the quarry with cottages behind. Other Rowley Regis photographs include Hailstone Quarry (A1939-42) and Central Quarry (A1943-4). The former had an inclined tramway to the Dudley Canal. Turner's Hill Quarries are still active in this area; others have been reclaimed and landscaped.

Jack Rhodes, July 1921 [A1949] SO 969876

Jaw-crusher at Hailstone Quarry, Rowley Regis

A good close-up view, but of specialist interest. This jaw-crusher is of the Blake-Marsden type, manufactured by Goodwin Barsby & Co. Photographs A1941-2 show the bucket elevator to raise the crushed stone to the trommels or cylindrical screens for grading. Hailstone Quarry was close to Prospect Quarry.
Jack Rhodes, July 1921 [A1940] SO 965880

Steam Plant at Prospect Quarry, Rowley Regis, Staffordshire (now West Midlands)

This quarry is 300 yards (274 metres) north-west of Rowley Regis church, and next to the larger Allsopps Hill Quarry. First setts and kerbs, and then roadstone have been worked here in the Rough Hills in a small intrusion of basalt which has narrow columnar jointing. The Rowley Basalt is a crushed band known locally as 'Rowley Rag'. In a corner at the south end of the quarry stands this boiler used for supplying steam for driving the rock-drill seen in the above photograph. The vertical boiler is portable, being rail-mounted, and was manufactured by John Thompson of Wolverhampton. The iron wagon must be a water tank for the boiler. Compare this with the steam plant in Dosthill Quarry.

Jack Rhodes, 1.15 p.m. July 1921 [A1948] SO 969876

CHAPTER ELEVEN
SAND & GRAVEL

SANDS AND GRAVELS ARE a major source of aggregates for roadstone, concrete and artificial stone. They are there for the taking without recourse to the blasting and crushing processes seen in the roadstone quarries; only screening and grading may be necessary on-site. Sands are quarried in pits in mostly Tertiary and later deposits, although some older sandstone beds may be unconsolidated or weak enough to be crushed, as we see at Gornal. According to its make-up, sand can be used for mortar, glass-making and foundry moulding sand. In Kent, the Thanet Sand was an important source for moulding sand, being quarried extensively around Woolwich for the home and export markets.

Sands and gravels are frequently found together. Those of recent origin include glacial deposits, as seen in Hertfordshire and Cumberland. Boulder clay often covers these in northern England (it also overlies the ironstone beds seen being worked at Wartnaby in Leicestershire). Alluvial sand and gravel deposits have been dug from pits in many places in the country, and there has been much activity in and around south-east England, an area with a high demanding market. The Thames Valley river gravels, for example, contain a high portion of flints. Large modern pits here have often been left

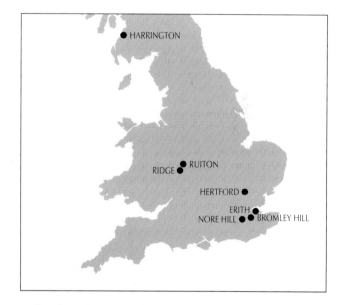

to flood, such as near Reading or further upstream around South Cerney, now designated the Cotswold Water Park. Flinty gravels from the older High Terrace of the lower Thames basin are seen being worked as a by-product of the Swanscombe chalk pits in Kent (Chapter Four).

93

Ruiton Sand Pit, Upper Gornal, Staffordshire

An edge runner stone for crushing 'Gornal Sandstone' is the point of interest here. Held by a central pivot, the crusher would be turned in a circle by a horse (not working in this picture). The runner stone's diameter and weight have been increased by adding wood, surrounded by a thick iron tyre. The Gornal Sandstone (Old Red Sandstone) is an inlier of about 35 feet (11 metres) of yellow-buff stone. Several older buildings of local sandstone survive in this area, including those in this view: the Ruiton United Reformed (formerly Independent) Chapel of 1830, and the Sunday School building behind the runner-stone. Today, the upper part of the quarry has houses on it, while the lower part remains as a shallow depression in an open area of rough grazing. There were similar small workings around here, now mostly built-over. The quarry is about 1 mile (1.6 km) north-west of Dudley. Rhodes says this view is looking south; it is actually looking north.

Jack Rhodes, July 1921 [A1968] SO 919921

Ridge sand pit, near Stourbridge, Worcestershire

An old man stands in this small pit which shows tool marks in the soft sandstone face. Pockets of gravel are being worked at the junction of the Bunter Pebble beds with the lower Mottled Sandstones (Triassic). The view is looking east and the location is 'about 30 yards west of the Foresters Arms Inn, near Stourbridge.' The pub survives beside the A458 at Wollaston and there are various old workings here and along the wooded ridge.

Jack Rhodes, July 1922 [A2198] SO 883848

Parish's Loam Works, Erith, Kent

This view of the south portion of the great pit, 'entered along the southern tramline,' shows how the method of working has created such a bizarre scene. A small adit (tunnel) is made at the foot of the face and the overlying sand is shovelled down into a wagon placed at the mouth of the adit, a method similar to that seen at the Swanscombe chalk quarry. The whole thickness of the Thanet Sand (Eocene), about 70 feet (21 metres), is seen here. Despite the summer month and time of day, this particular occasion must have been dull, for Rhodes used a 2-second exposure for the photograph.

Jack Rhodes, 11.30 a.m. 27 June 1911
?TQ 503782

Gravel pit, near Hertford, Hertfordshire

Men are 'working with spades, sieves and barrows at a face which gives a fine section of well-bedded glacial sand and gravel beneath a chalky boulder clay. The view is looking south, and the location of this pit was ³/₄ mile east of River Lea Bridge, Hertford,' which would be at Balls Hill. Photograph A1930 shows another gravel pit north-west of Ware station at TL 348148.

Jack Rhodes, 2.50 p.m. May 1921 [A1932]
TL 336127

Bromley Hill gravel pit, Kent

A steam dragline crane is working in a field on the east side of Bromley Hill, extracting the Blackheath Pebble Beds for making concrete. The Bucyrus crane is rail-mounted, on double bogies. It is a dragline - its bucket drawing the gravel towards the crane - and shows a degree of sophistication with wire ropes for raising and lowering the jib and bucket; the digging rope draws the bucket in and releases it. Gravel is dropped into the hopper which stands over the end of a narrow-gauge tramway. In the foreground, and partly hiding the crane, note the 'grizzley' with a sloping frame with iron bars for grading the gravel by size. A 2-second exposure was used for this photograph, as at Parish's Loam Works ten years before. Photograph A1924 shows a sand pit, also on the east side of Bromley Hill.

Jack Rhodes, 12.30 p.m. June 1921 [A1921]
site not located

Nore Hill gravel pits, Worms Heath, Surrey

The pit is worked in disturbed pebble beds on the west side of Worms Heath, about 1½ miles (2.4 kilometres) south-east of Warlingham. The view, looking east, gives a good idea of the depth of the deposit or solution hollows in the chalk in which it occurs. Two lorries are loading at the back. Both have solid tyres and their drivers have placed their coats over the radiators to keep them warm on this winter's day. The righthand lorry is owned by T. Scott & Sons of nearby Warlingham. The other one belongs to Henry Streeter, contractor of Croydon; it is shown in more detail in photograph A5378, taken to show 'rafts' of angular flints within the mass of pebbles.

Jack Rhodes, December 1930 [A5377]
TQ 378576

Gravel pit at Harrington, near Workington, Cumberland

In contrast, a photograph of a pit worked in glacial sand and gravel in the north-west of England. A steam crane is seen on rails and a portable steam engine works the screening plant. Note also the two horses and carts. This pit is located 'below Harrington station,' a rather unhelpful description as there were two stations with adjacent gravel pits at the time! It is probably the one on the coast railway, which is still open.

Jack Rhodes, August 1922 [A2292]
?NX 991254

CHAPTER TWELVE
SANDSTONE

SANDSTONES OF DIFFERENT COMPOSITION, texture and colour occur widely in England and Wales. Devonian sandstones (Old Red Sandstone) have yielded flagstones for building and paving in north Devon and the Welsh Borders, but the oldest shown here are the sandstones of Carboniferous age. The Pennant sandstones of the Upper Coal Measures have been of local significance around Bristol, the Forest of Dean and south Wales, but quarries in the sandstones of the Millstone Grit and Lower Coal Measures were far more widespread in the Pennine areas, especially in Derbyshire, Lancashire and Yorkshire. Many quarries provided building and paving stones for the expanding industrial towns of these counties in the nineteenth century and millstones, grindstones, scythestones and pulpstones were wrought from the harder gritstones.

The stone of west Yorkshire has been of such importance that York Stone is the name given to the product from its quarries. The many types include the Rough Rock which was quarried extensively in Victorian times for buildings in Halifax, Huddersfield and more distant towns. Local names for the Rough Rock include Brambley Fall Stone and Crosland Hill Stone. Some remarkable quarries were opened in the Rough Rock in a concentrated area around Crosland Hill on Crosland Moor, 2 miles (3.2 kilometres) south-west of

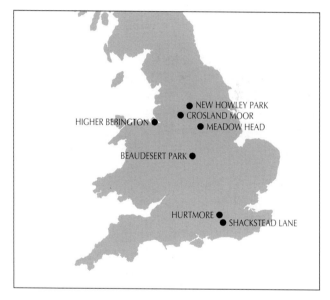

Huddersfield. In addition to the photographs shown here, there are five other quarries depicted in the BGS collection, accounting for at least fifteen steam cranes. Today, the main quarriers are Johnsons Wellfield Quarries Ltd, with large stoneworks and four quarries. The Rough Rock Flags were quarried as 'Greetland Stone' at Greetland near Halifax. The important Elland Flags produced roof tiles, paving slabs and architectural and monumental stone; the stone was also mined in places (Godwin, 1984). The Greenmoor Rock and Grenoside Sandstone are the equivalents further south in the Sheffield area.

Bunter and Keuper sandstones of the Triassic (New Red Sandstone) are found across the West Midlands and Staffordshire, passing into Shropshire, Cheshire and Lancashire, as well as through Nottinghamshire into Yorkshire. Among the noted varieties suitable for building are the freestones exploited at Grinshill in Shropshire. The Keuper sandstone quarried at Runcorn was said to be the best in Cheshire, while there were other quarries at Lymm and Weston. At Storeton on the Wirral, Lower Keuper Sandstone forms a north-south ridge from Oxton to Higher Bebington, where deep quarries were worked. The quarry photographed here produced a light red sandstone, no longer available, while on the Lancashire side of the Mersey, duller sandstones were quarried at Woolton and Rainhill for Liverpool's new Anglican cathedral. New Red Sandstones were an important source of building stone for the developing towns of the western Midlands in the nineteenth century. In Staffordshire, Hollington Quarry near Uttoxeter was the source of a famous sandstone, with both 'white' and 'red' varieties; the latter chosen for the new Coventry Cathedral. From the same county we see a good example of a quarry at Beaudesert Park.

Younger sandstones of variable quality have been exploited locally for building in parts of the south of England. For example, Kentish Rag from the Hythe Beds of the Lower Greensand (Cretaceous) was quarried at Hythe, Sandgate, Basted and Offham. It was used by the Romans and in medieval times. Stone from the main quarries around Maidstone was shipped in barges via the Medway and Thames to London and Windsor. The outcrop of the Wealden Lower Greensand has yielded building sand and silica sand from the Folkestone Beds and high quality Fuller's Earth from the underlying Sandgate Beds. Below these and to the west of Dorking, the Bargate Beds contain a dark brown calcareous sandstone. Bargate Stone is the best-known of the Surrey sandstones and was quarried in a small way near Godalming. It was used to face the walls of Guildford Castle in the twelfth century and much later at Charterhouse School; Sir Edwin Lutyens used it in nearby country houses in the early twentieth century.

'Firestone' from the Upper Greensand was worked in drift mines following the dip of the beds beneath the chalk in the east of Surrey. This was Reigate Stone, a hard calcareous variety of freestone used for building, both locally and as far as London. Many mines around Reigate, at Chaldon, Merstham, Godstone and Brockham were re-worked in the nineteenth and early twentieth centuries for the softer 'Hearthstone', used for whitening steps and floors.

New Howley Park Quarry, Morley, Yorkshire

Thornhill Rock, a Carboniferous sandstone, has been much quarried around Morley and Dewsbury where it was sometimes called Howley Park Stone. This is in fact the New Bluestone Quarry, worked in 1925 by 49 men under the employ of George Armitage & Sons Ltd. In the dressing yard, a large block is being lifted by a steam derrick with a short fixed jib, while a steam crane on rails handles a sawn slab - other slabs are stacked in the foreground. There must be a frame saw nearby but a planing machine is just visible in the shed behind. The railway on the right is a siding from the main line; the board at the far end of the track reads: 'LNER NO ENGINE MUST PASS THIS [POINT]'. There is good reason, for the deep quarry is immediately beyond. It was worked below the overlying shales which were used for making bricks (see page 22), and the brickworks chimney is seen rising behind the shed roof. The mineral railway ran to other stone saw mills and quarries at Britannia, Finsadale, Howley Park and Rein Road.
Jack Rhodes, July 1926 [A3614] SE 261257

Spinkwell Quarry, Crosland Moor, near Huddersfield, Yorkshire

Looking north-east across a large face of the Upper Freestone bed of the Rough Rock which is being worked along prominent joint faces. The working section of the quarry is served by the two steam cranes. Note the swivelling tipper wagons or bogies for removing waste at two levels inside the quarry on the left, where waste has been stacked behind drystone walls. The dressing sheds surround a workyard, with a small crushing plant for dealing with waste stone on the extreme right. A traditional timber hand-derrick with a long luffing jib stands beside a lorry which is owned by J. Wimpenny & Co., the quarriers who employed nineteen men here and another four at the smaller Guy Edge Quarry at Linthwaite. Although the picture is dominated by three cranes, there is evidence for seven others here and at nearby works.
Jack Rhodes, July 1926 [A3592] SE 118148

Whitefield Quarry, Crosland Moor

Three elderly quarrymen pose proudly beside a wheelbarrow. The Rough Rock beds here were more flaggy than usual and the beds and joints have made a broken and overhanging face, hence the ladders all of different lengths which have been arranged to reach the quarry floor. The small building at the top may be a smithy. Rhodes described this as 'Normington & Co's Quarry, Crosland Moor.' G.H. Normington & Co. employed sixteen men here in 1925.

Jack Rhodes, July 1926 [A3603] location uncertain

J. Shaw & Sons' Quarry, Crosland Moor

A large quarry in the freestone bed (Rough Rock), served by two modern derrick-cranes with lattice steel jibs. The uppermost beds consist of gritstone ('tiger') and are too tough to work for building purposes. Note how the quarry is being worked in small benches along horizontal bedding planes in the rock, and the overburden and waste is discarded on the left. The electric-powered crane on the left works the quarry and looks new, for the sides of the cab are pine-boarded and appear unpainted.

Stone slabs placed behind the cab act as a counterweight. The crane is about to lift an open skip loaded with waste from the workyard onto the tip on the left. The other crane handles stock in the open yard and seems to be counterweighted by an old steam boiler behind the cab. It is supported by three stays, one of which is lattice steel. A curious arrangement with the lefthand timber stay allows the additional use of a smaller crane here. Large sawn slabs are stacked below the jib, so there must be a frame saw in the sheds on the right.

Various other stone items can be seen in the yard. The high corrugated iron wall on the right was no doubt erected for protection against the weather, but it unfortunately screens details of the workyard area. Photograph A3600 shows men removing the overburden, wheeling barrows over a plank above the stone face. It is unclear if this is Old Park or Old Spinkwell Quarry, as both are recorded as being worked in 1925 by Joe Shaw & Sons Ltd.

Jack Rhodes, July 1926 [A3599] SE 119148 or SE 116146

Chapelfield Quarry, Crosland Moor

Worked by Thomas Bower & Co. Note the large steam crane on a massive stone foundation block. The overburden here is relatively shallow, and the men are removing a harder coarser grained gritstone to gain the Rough Rock freestone. The top of a good bed has been exposed and is being cleaned off. Waste stone is placed in the low-sided skips for disposal. Sizable blocks lie among the waste which can be seen back-filling the quarry on the left foreground. Other large blocks are stacked at the surface beside the crane and some show marks where they have been split by cutting grooves and inserting wedges. The view is looking east towards the backs of houses along Blackmoorfoot Road; three houses appear to be newly built.

Jack Rhodes, July 1926 [A3608] SE 119150

Flagstone Quarry, Meadow Head, Sheffield

Looking north-west over a shallow but busy quarry, with cranes and men working at several locations. The stone is the Brincliff Edge Rock from the Lower Coal Measures, 30 feet (9.1 metres) thick and covered by black shales, and worked here for flagstones and ashlar. The steam crane in the foreground has a short, fixed jib which can be passed under both stays. The crane at New Howley Park is similar, although this one has a shelter for the driver. The nearby timber hand-crane has a similar arrangement, and the shed next to it houses a stone saw. A true hand-derrick in the background has a luffing jib and horizontal sleepers between the stays to aid its stability. Note the masons at work in the foreground, squaring blocks in the open air. In 1911, it was recorded that F. Tinker employed four men at Meadow Head Quarry, producing clay and sandstone, apparently connected with a factory. By 1925, the Meadow Head Brick & Stone Works Ltd had just two men in the quarry. The site lies near Norton Woodseats within the southern suburbs of Sheffield.

Jack Rhodes, 2.30 p.m. 5 May 1911 [A1131] SK 346822

Higher Bebington Quarry, Storeton, Cheshire (now Merseyside)

A pinkish Lower Keuper Sandstone is being worked here in this deep quarry on the Wirral peninsula. Work is proceeding on a new bench, using a steam channeller with a horizontal boiler. Having been lifted into position by crane and mounted on its own short railway track, this machine is using percussive steel blades to cut down vertically to about 10 feet (3 metres) in two cuts, one on each side. Grooves channelled at right angles can be seen just to the left. Wedges inserted in horizontal holes along the natural bedding of the sandstone allow large rectangular blocks to be extracted. Note the cutting marks left on the faces as the excavation has progressed downwards, so characteristic of this method of quarrying dimension stone. The face below the channeller shows hollows or cavities of weaker rock supported by timbers. Access to the working area is by solid timber steps built in stages as the quarry deepens. The scene is dominated by a large steam crane which has recently raised the quarried stones seen atop the platform of blocks. Note also the worksheds and the proximity of terraced houses behind. Charles Wells of Bootle employed seventeen men here in 1914, but the Great War is just two months away. Frank Wells took over after the war, and worked the quarry until the early 1960s, producing dimensional stone and silica sand. As at other quarries in the district, this one has the 'Footprint Bed' which contains casts of reptiles, as well as impressions of ripple-marks and plant remains (Herdman, 1903, 222). The $2\frac{1}{2}$ mile (4 km) Storeton Tramway was opened in 1838 from the quarries to a stone quay on the Mersey at Bromborough Pool (now Port Sunlight). It had closed by 1905, so was no longer in use at the time of this photograph.

Jack Rhodes, 1.30 p.m. June 1914 [A1675]
SJ 316843

Beaudesert Park Quarry, near Rugeley, Staffordshire

The quarry is near the 'electric light works' in Beaudesert Park and about 150 yards (137 metres) north-west of Beaudesert Hall, home of the Pagets. Sandstone from the upper band of the Lower Keuper Sandstone (Triassic) is being quarried for alterations at the hall, but the result of this activity was short-lived, alas, for the building was demolished in 1932-5. Overlying the sandstone is the base bed of the Keuper Marl, and the crane uses this solid geological division to support its two stays in a rather cramped site. The crane itself is of a traditional nineteenth-century type which could have been manufactured locally. The jib is fixed and the crane lifts out blocks for initial working at an intermediate level. Waste is discarded and the valuable stone is lifted out by a crane stationed at the surface (its chain and hook are hanging on the right). Note the pick marks visible in the quarry face, where quarriers have made vertical channels to shape out blocks. In the bottom corner a block has been separated and divided in two by a channel. The quarrymen have then chiselled out short horizontal grooves for inserting wedges to lift the block along a potential weakness (a practice where there is no well-defined bed). Because of rather dull conditions, Rhodes was obliged to use a 24-second exposure for this photograph which looks south-east. The time of day would suggest this was during the men's lunch-break, thus explaining their absence.

Jack Rhodes, 1 p.m. 11 October 1912 [A1543]
SK 053134

'Jumping' at Shackstead Lane Quarry, Godalming, Surrey

This shows the curious method of quarrying the Bargate stone. 'Doggers' of the calcareous sandstone are prized out of the Bargate Beds by long crowbars, with extra leverage obtained by placing a 10-foot (3 metre) plank at right angles to the bar, with one end on the ground. In this picture, five quarrymen stand ready to jump in unison on the plank, balancing themselves with long poles. Crude, but it worked! Note also the raised plankway for the wheelbarrows removing overburden. The quarry lay on the south side of Shackstead Lane, to the south of the town.

Jack Rhodes, October 1926 [A3813]
SU 965430

Hurtmore Quarry, near Godalming, Surrey

The Bargate Beds of sand and calcareous sandstone are seen in the exposed face of this quarry which is worked by hand in tiers or benches. The internal transport is by wheelbarrows using a precarious raised plankway on the right, similar to those seen in the ironstone workings on page 50. The six men at the bottom of the quarry are 'jumping' a stone, an action shown in detail in the photograph at Shackstead Lane Quarry. Note the jumping bar propped to the right of the ladder on the middle bench. Quarried stone waits to be passed up from bench to bench to the surface, where piles of stone are ready to be dressed, producing slabs for crazy paving, roadstone and small rectangular blocks suitable for builders. Hurtmore Quarry, about 1½ miles (2.4 kilometres) north-west of Godalming, was being worked by F. Milton & Sons Ltd at the time of this photograph. Looking east by north.

Jack Rhodes, October 1926 [A3814]
SU 950452

Corwen Slate Mine, Penarth, Merionethshire (now Clwyd)

Also known as Penarth Quarry. A true slate landscape here, where the slate was worked underground, two miles (3.2 km) east of Corwen. Everything is slate, apart from the window frames, glass and iron tramway rails. The view is looking east. In the foreground, slates of different sizes are stacked ready for dispatch on a terrace beside a dressing shed, at the end of which two men are standing in a mine entrance. Another long shed is on a higher terrace set into the extensive waste tips. Note how the waste is held back by skilfully-built drystone walls, typical of the Welsh slate quarries where large quantities of material had to be discarded on a confined site. Through the centre passes a steep incline, worked from the sturdy winding house clinging to the mountainside, top right. This is the top of a half-mile (0.8 km) tramway which descended north-west to the Penarth Slate Wharf, where there were sidings and a sawmill beside the Llangollen and Corwen Railway. Although slate had been worked earlier, the main developments here came in 1876 after the railway had been opened. Only slate slabs were being produced when the mine closed in 1932.

Jack Rhodes, July 1925 [A3119] SJ 109424

CHAPTER THIRTEEN
SLATE

SLATE IS A METAMORPHIC rock of the west, formed by the action of great pressure and heat on sedimentary mudstones and shales. The resulting characteristic cleavage planes lie at right angles to that pressure and give this durable rock the facility to be split into thin slabs. The most fissile varieties can be split extremely thinly, so that over the centuries quarrymen have produced millions of strong but lightweight roofing slates or tiles. In addition, slate slabs have been used for flooring, cisterns, tables and lintels.

A distinction must be made between these true slates and the much heavier 'slates' obtained from local thin-bedded sandstones and limestones for use as roofing tiles. Those include, for example, the gritstone Kerridge Slabs from near Macclesfield in Cheshire, or the Collyweston and Stonesfield 'slates' of Northamptonshire and Oxfordshire. The picturesque stone roofs of the Cotswold villages are among the best known (see page 69), but many other places have their own style, such as in the Purbeck district of Dorset (page 72).

The greatest period of slate production was the second half of the nineteenth century, when the most important source was the Snowdonia district of north Wales, in the former counties of Caernarvonshire and Merionethshire. The main quarrying centres were in Cambrian slates at Bethesda (Penrhyn), Llanberis (Dinorwig) and Nantlle, and underground

in Ordovician slates around Blaenau Ffestiniog (Lindsay, 1974). The BGS collection does not include these famous slate quarries and mines, but the photographs presented here are of a group of workings north of the Berwyn Mountains around Corwen and Llangollen on the Denbighshire and Merionethshire borders (now Clwyd). These were in Silurian strata containing mudstones, siltstones and flags, and the larger quarries relied upon tramway connections to a canal or railway for the onward transport of their products. Other Welsh slates of Ordovician age were worked in Pembrokeshire and Carmarthenshire (Dyfed).

In England, numerous slate quarries were worked around the Lake District counties of Cumberland and Lancashire (now Cumbria), although never on the grand scale of Snowdonia. The slate here is mainly of Ordovician age and includes the green Borrowdale series which are composed of volcanic ash. The chosen photograph shows Burlington Quarry at Kirkby, where a grey-blue Silurian slate is still worked. Even older Pre-Cambrian slates were quarried in the Charnwood Forest of Leicestershire, although on a small scale.

South-west England is also represented in the photographs, where Devonian slates have long been quarried for building and roofing materials. The most important district was in north Cornwall around Delabole and along the cliffs at Trebarwith and Tintagel. There are records of the quarrying and shipping of slates since at least medieval times. The most famous quarry is at Delabole, worked for centuries and considerably expanded since the eighteenth century so that it is now the deepest slate quarry in England. Other parts of Cornwall produced roofing slates, such as at St Neot near Liskeard, where the stone was worked in underground caverns. Slates were quarried in south Devon near Kingsbridge, and in the west around Tavistock. Near Plymouth, Cann Quarry was famous for its slate, although BGS photograph A398 was taken to show an elvan (igneous) dyke here (Ussher, 1912, Plate IV).

Tramway wagons at Deeside Slab Quarry

Roofing slates are seen carefully loaded on two sturdily-built wagons with dumb buffers. Note the straw sheaves, brought up for packing the finished slates. Empties were hauled up the Deeside Tramway by horses in the morning, but gravity was used for the downward journey at the end of the day. Loaded wagons were run down individually carrying one or two men, the speed controlled by the diagonal screw-down brakes at the side. The 2 foot 7 inches (0.76 metre) gauge tramway was built about 1840 or 1850 to connect the Deeside Slab Quarry with its mill at Nant-y-Pandy. In 1876/7 it was extended at each end, to the north to Glyndyfrdwy station on the Llangollen-Corwen section of the GWR (opened 1868), where latterly a gantry transferred the slates in crude wooden containers to main line wagons. An incline rose from here, after which the track continued past the mill to climb steeply for 2 miles (3.6 km) to the slab quarries. The tramway was unusual in that on the original section the rails were made of timber, faced with a narrow running surface of iron. From the slab quarry the southwards extension, like the north, was laid with conventional rails. This ran for another mile (1.6 km) via two inclines to the more exposed Moelfferna slate quarry and mine higher up at 1,600 feet (488 metres). Although the slab quarry closed in 1923, Moelfferna continued to be served by the tramway until 1950 before it too closed ten years later. The slates seen here must be from Moelfferna.

Jack Rhodes, July 1925 [A3118] SJ 138405

Deeside Slab Quarry, near Glyndyfrdwy, Merionethshire (now Clwyd)

The quarry was opened 1,200 feet (366 metres) up in the Berwyn Mountains sometime in or after the 1840s. Products were used for making beer and whisky vats, water cisterns, troughs and laboratory slabs. The view shows part of the 'Slab Horizon' of the Glyn-Dyfrdwy group of the Lower Ludlow series (Silurian), with rapidly alternating bands of cleaved mudstone and uncleaved laminated silt. The rock splits between the cleaved and uncleaved layers into slabs of uniform thickness, which can be seen on the floor in the foreground. The tripod shearlegs has a simple hand winch on the left and is held steady by two chains anchored to the face behind. Shotholes for blasting are visible as short pale strokes on the right hand face. The older waste tips on the left look dangerously close to the quarry edge. Note also the tramways leading to waste tips and the Deeside Tramway. The scene depicts a quarry which had closed two years earlier.
Jack Rhodes, July 1925 [A3116] SJ 138404

Deeside Slate Works, Glyndyfrdwy

Slate slabs were brought here for dressing and finishing in this works which was established in a sheltered valley beside a stream, about 1½ miles (2.4 km) down the tramway from the Deeside Slab Quarry. This picture clearly demonstrates the importance of water power at remote mountain sites, and looks east over a large waterwheel which was the main source of power for the sawing and planing machinery in the long slate-roofed dressing shed on the left. This wheel has a diameter of 30 feet (9.1 metres), the power being transferred by the geared ring drive. Note also the small iron hand-crane in the yard below and slate slabs leaning against the small building behind. The slate works is said to have been closed by 1914; the wheel, which was backshot, is disused in this photograph as the launder bringing water from the left has been removed.
Jack Rhodes, July 1925 [A3121] SJ 148418

Sawing shed at Wynne Slate Quarry, Glyn Ceiriog, Denbighshire (now Clwyd)

Further slate quarries were opened in the remoter Ceiriog valley 3 miles (4.8 km) south-south-west of Llangollen, where the Cambrian and Wynne quarries at Glyn Ceiriog were enlarged in the 1870s, with underground work from the 1890s. These developments were made possible by the Glyn Valley Tramroad (1873-1935), to which both quarries were connected by inclines. The 2 foot 4¼ inch (0.72 metre) tramway ran for 6 miles (9.6 km) to a wharf at Gledrid on the Shropshire Union (Ellesmere) Canal. It was horse-drawn until

1888, when a link was made to Chirk railway station and steam locomotives were introduced (Milner, 1984). In this photograph, four young workers and their supervisor pose inside the sawing shed of the Wynne Slate Quarry. They stand between the tables of two sawing machines for preparing slates for splitting. As with the larger machine seen at Delabole Quarry in Cornwall, the slate is moved forwards on a bed to meet the saw, although in this case the circular blade is fixed below the bed. Spare blades can be seen on the left. The lad in the front holds a mallet and chisel, the tools for splitting slates by hand. In the background on

the left are two rotary trimmers with wire safety guards, for trimming and squaring split slates to size. This type of machine, which is still in use today, was invented in 1856 by J. W. Greaves of Llechwedd Quarry, Blaenau Ffestiniog. He also invented a sawing table. This interior is typical of many slate-dressing sheds, which were long low buildings with thick timbers supporting a roof with a wide span. Skylight windows let in light and discarded slate lies everywhere. The building has been demolished but the Wynne Quarry site has a small museum and underground tours for visitors.

Jack Rhodes. July 1925 [A3108] SJ 201379.

Clogau Quarries, Oernant, Denbighshire (now Clwyd)

This is a spectacular piece of man-sculptured landscape, showing beds from the same horizon seen at the Deeside Slab Quarry. The near-vertical cleavage gives the dramatic effect. The jib of a small fixed crane can be seen just behind the unquarried block of poorer quality slate. Clogau, or Berwyn Quarry, is at the Horseshoe Pass in the Llantysilio Mountain range on the north side of the Dee valley. This view looks north-north-west across the main quarry, and the sloping flank of Gribin Oernant is in the background. Transport was facilitated in 1852 when the 3 feet (0.9 metre) gauge Oernant Tramway was opened from the Oernant and Clogau quarries down to Pentrefelin on the Llangollen Canal, where a water-powered slate works (with planers, saws and a polisher) was in use until the 1920s. The throwing of waste slate into the River Dee was always a problem here. The tramway was extended northwards in 1857 to serve the Moel y Faen quarries, but the whole was disused by 1914. Clogau Quarry was also disused at that time, to be reopened in later years. In 1994, Berwyn Slate Quarries Ltd were working it as the Berwyn Quarry for slabs.

Jack Rhodes, July 1925 [A3125] SJ 185463

Coryton Slate Quarry, near Tavistock, Devon

A dramatic slate working where the bedding planes have been upturned so they dip steeply from right to left. The cleavage planes dip from left to right, giving the false impression of beds in this view. Two beds suitable for roofing slates have been quarried, separated by a broad leaning wall of inferior rock, with the effect that quarrying was semi-underground. The figure is standing in one excavated bed, while the second bed is hidden on the far side of the overhanging wall. The quarry was last worked in 1925 by three men in the employ of Herbert Petherick. Now worked out and flooded, it lies in a wood one mile (1.6 km) west of Coryton church, 6 miles (9.6 km) north-north-west of Tavistock. Several other slate quarries were worked in this district, at Lewtrenchard, Bridestowe, Sourton, Stowford and Lifton. This picture was published in Reid, *et al* (1911, Plate II).

T. Clifford Hall, not dated, c.1908/9 [A815] SX 440835

Delabole Quarry, north Cornwall

A view from about a third of the way down the main six-tracked incline into this celebrated quarry, then about 450 feet (137 metres) deep. The dip of the cleavage in the slate can be clearly seen in the distant face. The quarry is being worked in benches, the deepest part being served by the lefthand pair of incline tracks. The tramways branch to the numerous working faces, and empty and loaded wagons can be seen at the foot of the inclines. The righthand incline track reappears centre-right, where there are four shearlegs for loading stone and a stationary steam engine. At least eight more shearlegs can be seen, while four rail-mounted steam cranes are working on the two lowest levels. It must have been difficult getting these down into the quarry. Note the launders bringing water to the waterwheels which worked pumps further down the hole for drawing water up to the main drainage adit. The steep incline was about 300 yards (274 metres) long and quarried slate was hauled up for splitting, dressing or tipping out on the huge waste tips to the south and east. At least five steam engines performed the winding and worked some of the machinery. Slate was also drawn out by a system of aerial ropeways rising to timber structures known as the 'papote heads'. These were stationed at the top of the quarry just to the left of this view. Grey slate has been quarried at Delabole since at least Elizabethan times, and this enormous excavation results from the amalgamation of four or five smaller quarries which began to expand in the eighteenth century. Roofing slates for export to southern England and even the continent were taken by carts and wagons and loaded onto sailing vessels drawn up on the beach at the small harbours of Port Gaverne and Port Isaac. Much of this changed with the opening of the North Cornwall Railway in 1893, when a direct siding was made into the slate works above the quarry. The photograph shows the railway embankment passing close to the edge of the quarry (top left).

T. Clifford Hall, 12.15 p.m. 14 September 1907 [A505] SX 075840

Slate blocks near the main incline head at Delabole, looking north-west

Large slate blocks are seen chained to wagons, having been brought up to the incline head, which is around to the right beyond the picture. They are about to enter the end of the long trimming and splitting shed on the left. Power for the machinery here is transmitted by a drive shaft supported on a pillar as it crosses from the power house. The tower was formerly the accumulator for a hydraulic power system which was apparently never used. Curiously, in a place where slate was so readily at hand, the end of one building is built of bricks. Note also the steel chimney. Another dressing shed is seen behind the power house. Through the gap, roofing slates are stacked ready for export.

The history of the development of the quarry, its waste tips, engine houses and dressing sheds is extremely complex. The original 3 feet (0.9 metre) gauge of the quarry's extensive tramway system was replaced in 1890 by one of 1 foot 11 inches (0.57 metre), and the main incline was changed from four tracks to six. Horses worked inside the quarry and at the surface, where they were aided by two (later three) steam locomotives. The dressing sheds were built on the extensive waste tips. John Jenkin (1888) gives a useful account of Delabole, while a novel by Eden Phillpotts (1915) describes the quarry at the time of expansion in the late nineteenth century. At the time of these photographs, the Old Delabole Slate Co. Ltd. employed 408 men (148 inside and 260 outside). Today, there are less than a hundred.

T. Clifford Hall, 2.30 p.m. 14 September 1907
[A507] SX 075835

Sawing table at Delabole

As happened at quarries elsewhere, not all Delabole slate was split for roofing slate, and the view shows a sawing table with two big circular blades for producing flooring slabs. Although not at work in this picture, slate blocks would be placed on a moving bed to pass beneath the saw blades. The rim of each blade is fitted with thirty cutting tools - round steel rods with flattened heads and set in sockets so they can be renewed. The saw marks are clearly seen on the off-cuts upon which the worker is standing. This was a Hunter saw, invented in 1856, and the maker's name plate reads: 'HUNTER'S PATENT. WINTON & CO. ENGINEERS. CARNARVON 1856.' In 1888, Jenkin described 'three large hunter saws, a very great novelty to see working, and capable of sawing up the hardest blocks of a foot or more in thickness.' Note also the belt drives, unguarded, and the waste dust which shows the machine has been well used. It is sometimes difficult to imagine that fine products could emerge from a scene of such apparent disorder, but Delabole produced slate slabs for floors, cisterns, mantle-pieces, tomb-stones, lintels, window-sills and many other miscellaneous uses. Hall used a 30-second exposure for this indoor photograph.

T. Clifford Hall, 3.45 p.m. 14 September 1907 [A510] SX 075835

116

Fisher East End, Burlington Slate Quarries, Kirkby-in-Furness, Lancashire (now Cumbria)

Looking west across part of the extensive chain of quarries running south-west to north-east for about a mile (1.6 km) in the Burlington range, producing a blue-grey slate from the Silurian Lower Flags. The best slate was not reached until a depth of 50 feet (15 metres) and the method of working was to open a line of quarries at intervals. These eventually joined up, but 'sinks' were meanwhile sunk in each quarry floor to exploit deeper beds. All these levels were served by tramways which took the slate out through tunnels to the dressing sheds or the massive waste tips outside. The main quarry seen here is the Fisher Sink. Balance lifts were used for raising the slate from the sinks. In the foreground, a horse-drawn tramway emerges from the Fisher Tunnel (right) to the heads of a vertical lift and, hidden beneath the roof, an inclined lift. Above the roof can be seen a smaller vertical lift for raising slate 30 feet (9 metres) from the Rachel Floor which is being opened inside the main Fisher Sink. A tunnel takes the tramway from the Fisher level through the unquarried mass of Smith Hill Main to the Town Sink beyond. The wall above that is the Town Main, which hides the quarries beyond. The history of the quarries has been described by Geddes (1975).

Jack Rhodes, August-September 1935 [A6731] SD 247836

BIBLIOGRAPHY

Anon, obituary, *Procs Geol Assoc, 69*, 1958, 72-3

Barton, R. M. *A History of the Cornish China Clay Industry*, Truro, 1966

Benfield, E. *Purbeck Shop: a stoneworker's story of stone,* new edition, Southampton, 1990

Bezzant, N. *Out of the Rock...,* 1980

Bird, E. The effects of Quarry Waste Disposal on beaches on the Lizard peninsula, Cornwall, *Journal of the Trevithick Society, 14* (1987), 83-92.

Blagg, T. F. C. Building Stone in Roman Britain, in Parsons, D. (ed) *Stone Quarrying and Building in England AD43-1525*, Chichester, 1990, 33-50

Clifton-Taylor, A. *The Pattern of English Building*, 1972

Dines, H. G. and Edmunds, F. H. *The Geology of the Country around Reigate and Dorking*, 1933 (Memoir for Sheet 286)

Gallois, R. W. *British Regional Geology: The Wealden District*, 4th ed, 1965

Geddes, R. S. *Burlington Blue-Grey*, Kirkby, 1975

Godwin, C. G. *Mining in the Elland Flags: a forgotten Yorkshire industry*, BGS Report Vol.16, No.4, 1984

Greenwell, A. and Elsden, J. V. *Practical Stone Quarrying*, 1913

Hains, B. A. and Horton, A. *British Regional Geology: Central England*, 3rd edition, 1969

Herdman, W. A. et al, Investigation of the Fauna and Flora of the Trias of the British Isles - Report of committee, *Rep. British Assoc.* 1903, 219-223

Hill, J. B. and MacAlister, D. A. *Geology of Falmouth and Truro, and of the Mining District of Camborne and Redruth*, 1906 (Memoir for Sheet 352)

Hollingworth, S. E. and Taylor, J. H. *The Mesozoic Ironstones of England: The Northampton Sand Ironstone*, 1951

Hounsell, B. Portland and its Stone, *Mine and Quarry Engineering*, April 1952, 107-114

Hudson, K. *The Fashionable Stone*, Bath, 1971

Jenkin, J. *Delabole Slate Quarry: A Sketch by a Workman on the Quarry*, Launceston, 1888

Jope, E. M. The Saxon Building Stone Industries in South and Midland England, *Medieval Archaeology 8* (1964), 91-118

Kelly's Directory for Warwickshire (1912)

Lamplugh, G. W. et al, *The Geology of the Melton Mowbray district and south-east Nottinghamshire*, 1909 (Memoir for Sheet 142)

Lewis, M. J. T. *The Pentewan Railway*, Twelveheads, 2nd edition, 1981

Lindsay, J. *A History of the North Wales Slate Industry*, Newton Abbot, 1974

Livens, F. H. and Barnes, W. Recent Excavator Practice, *Procs Inst Mech Eng*, July 1920, 609-37

Major, J. K. and Watts, M. *Victorian and Edwardian Windmills and Watermills from old photographs*, 1977

Messenger, M. J. *North Devon Clay*, Twelveheads, 1982

Milner, W. J. *The Glyn Valley Tramway*, Oxford, 1984

Parsons, D. (ed) *Stone Quarrying and Building in England AD43-1525*, Chichester, 1990

Phillpotts, E. *Old Delabole*, 1915

Reid, C. et al, *Geology of the Country around Tavistock and Launceston*, 1911 (Memoir for Sheet 337)

Richardson, L. *The Geology of the Country around Moreton-in-Marsh*, 1929 (Memoir for Sheet 217)

Shaw, M. Dee Side Tramway, *Industrial Railway Record 137*, June 1994, 281–8

Smeaton, J. *A Narrative of the Construction of the Eddystone Lighthouse*, 1791

Smith, J. R. *Cornwall's China Clay Heritage*, Twelveheads, 1992

Sowan, P. W. Firestone and Hearthstone Mines in the Upper Greensand of East Surrey, *Procs Geol Assoc*, 86, pt 4, 1975, 571-91

Stanier, P. *Quarries and Quarrying*, Princes Risborough, 1985

Stanier, P. The Granite Quarrying Industry in Devon and Cornwall: Part One, 1800-1910, *Industrial Archaeology Review*, VII, No.2 (1985), 171-89

Stanier, P. John Freeman and the Cornish Granite Industry 1840-1965, *Journal of the Trevithick Society* 13 (1986), 7-35

Ussher, W. A. E. *Geology of the Country around Ivybridge and Modbury*, 1912 (Memoir for Sheet 349)

Wade, E. A. *The Redlake Tramway and China Clay Works*, Twelveheads, 1982

Wallis, A. M. The Portland Stone Quarries, *Proc Dorset Nat Hist & Arch Soc* 12 (1891), 187-194

Williams, M. *The Slate Industry*, Princes Risborough, 1991

Williams, R. *Limekilns and Limeburning*, Princes Risborough, 1989

ACKNOWLEDGEMENTS

I am especially grateful to Graham McKenna, Chief Librarian of the British Geological Survey at Keyworth, for help in answering queries and access to papers about the early photographers; also Tim Cullen, photographer, and Dr Timothy Dhonau, who have both aided this project.

Many have given generously of their time and advice, but special praise must go to Michael Messenger and Alan Kittridge of Twelveheads Press, without whom this book would not have come to fruition. Mention must also be made of John Crompton, John England, J.S. Oxford, E. Pushman, Geoffrey Starmer and Merfyn Williams. Various quarriers and firms kindly allowed access to their sites, and lastly I am grateful for the services of the Cornish Studies Library, Clwyd Record Office, Gwynedd Record Office, Huddersfield Central Library, Nottingham Library, University of Southampton Geography Department and the Warwickshire Record Office.

INDEX